UTILITARIANISM
for and against

J. J. C. SMART
Emeritus Professor, University of Adelaide
Reader in Philosophy, La Trobe University

BERNARD WILLIAMS
Knightbridge Professor of Philosophy
University of Cambridge

CAMBRIDGE

at the University Press

1973

Published by the Syndics of the Cambridge University Press
Bentley House, 220 Euston Road, London NW1 2DB
American Branch: 32 East 57th Street, New York, N.Y. 10022

© Cambridge University Press 1973

Library of Congress Catalogue Card Number: 73–80487

ISBNs:
0 521 20297 3 hard covers
0 521 09822 X paperback

Printed in Great Britain
by Cox & Wyman Ltd,
London, Fakenham and Reading

Contents

An outline of a system of utilitarian ethics
J. J. C. SMART

A critique of utilitarianism
BERNARD WILLIAMS

J. J. C. SMART

An outline of a system of
utilitarian ethics

J. J. C. SMART

1. Introductory

Such writers as J. S. Mill, H. Sidgwick and G. E. Moore, as a result of philosophical reflection, produced systems of normative ethics. Of recent years normative ethics has become distinguished from meta-ethics, which discusses the nature of ethical concepts. Indeed, as a result of the prevalence of 'non-cognitivist' theories of meta-ethics, for example those of C. L. Stevenson[1] and R. M. Hare,[2] normative ethics has fallen into some disrepute, at any rate as a philosophical discipline. For non-cognitivist theories of ethics imply that our ultimate ethical principles depend on our ultimate attitudes and preferences. Ultimate ethical principles therefore seem to lie within the fields of personal decision, persuasion, advice and propaganda, but not within the field of academic philosophy.

While it is true that some ultimate ethical disagreements may depend simply on differences of ultimate preference, and while also the non-ultimate disagreements depend on differences about empirical facts, about which the philosopher is not specially qualified to judge, it nevertheless seems to me to be important to prevent this trend towards ethical neutrality of philosophy from going too far. The meta-ethical philosopher may far too readily forget that ordinary ethical thinking is frequently muddled, or else mixed up with questionable metaphysical assumptions. In the clear light of philosophical analysis some ethical systems may well come to seem less attractive. Moreover, even if there can be clear-headed disagreement about ultimate moral preferences, it is no small task to present one or other of the resulting ethical systems in a consistent and lucid manner, and in such a way as to show how

[1] *Ethics and Language* (Yale University Press, New Haven, 1944).
[2] *The Language of Morals* (Oxford University Press, London, 1952).

common, and often specious, objections to them can be avoided.

It will be my object in the present study to state a system of ethics which is free from traditional and theological associations. This is that type of utilitarianism which R. B. ✓Brandt has called 'act-utilitarianism'.[1] Roughly speaking, act-utilitarianism is the view that the rightness or wrongness of an action depends only on the total goodness or badness of its consequences, i.e. on the effect of the action on the welfare of all human beings (or perhaps all sentient beings). The best sustained exposition of act-utilitarianism is, I think, that in Sidgwick's *Methods of Ethics*,[2] but Sidgwick stated it within the framework of a cognitivist meta-ethics which supposed that the ultimate act-utilitarian principles could be known to be true by some sort of intellectual intuition. I reject Sidgwick's meta-ethics for familiar reasons, and for the purpose of this study will assume the truth of some such 'non-cognitivist' meta-ethical analysis as that of Hare's *Language of Morals*, or possibly that of D. H. Monro in his *Empiricism and Ethics*.[3] (Monro's theory should perhaps be classed as subjectivist rather than as non-cognitivist. However I am inclined to think that in the present state of linguistic theory it is not possible to make a very sharp distinction between these two sorts of theory.[4] For our present purposes the distinction is unimportant, because both sorts of theory imply that a man's ultimate ethical principles depend on his attitudes or feelings.) In adopting such a meta-ethics, I do, of course, renounce the attempt to

[1] See R. B. Brandt, *Ethical Theory* (Prentice-Hall, Englewood Cliffs, New Jersey, 1959), p. 380. Brandt distinguishes 'act' utilitarianism from 'rule' utilitarianism.

[2] H. Sidgwick, *Methods of Ethics*, 7th ed. (Macmillan, London, 1962).

[3] D. H. Monro, *Empiricism and Ethics* (Cambridge University Press, London, 1967).

[4] See my review of Monro's book, *Philosophical Review* 78 (1969) 259–61.

prove the act-utilitarian system. I shall be concerned with stating it in a form in which it may appear persuasive to some people, and to show how it may be defended against many of the objections which are frequently brought up against utilitarianism. Nevertheless I should like to indicate my opinion that the choice of conceptually clear and emotionally attractive systems of normative ethics which might be alternatives to it is not as wide as is sometimes thought.

In the first place, B. H. Medlin[1] has argued that it is impossible to state ethical egoism without either confusion or else a sort of pragmatic inconsistency. Secondly, some widespread ethical systems depend partly on metaphysical premises, and can therefore be undermined by philosophical criticism of these metaphysical bases. I myself would be prepared to argue that this is the case with respect to so-called 'natural law' ethics, which depends on a quasi-Aristotelian metaphysics. Thirdly, any system of deontological ethics, that is any system which does not appeal to the consequences of our actions, but which appeals to conformity with certain rules of duty, is open to a persuasive type of objection which may well be found convincing by some of those people who have the welfare of humanity at heart. For though, conceivably, in most cases the dictates of a deontological ethics might coincide with those of human welfare and of an act-utilitarian ethics, there must be some possible cases in which the dictates of the system clash with those of human welfare, indeed in which the deontological principles prescribe actions which lead to avoidable human misery. In the most attractive forms of deontological ethics the conflict with utilitarianism is in consequence of some principle of 'justice' or 'fairness', and I shall revert to this issue later.[2] In other cases,

[1] 'Ultimate principles and ethical egoism', *Australasian Journal of Philosophy* 35 (1957) 111–18.
[2] See pp. 67–73 below.

however, the conflict can be traced to some sort of confusion, perhaps even to some sort of superstitious 'rule worship'. There is *prima facie* a necessity for the deontologist to defend himself against the charge of heartlessness, in his apparently preferring abstract conformity to a rule to the prevention of avoidable human suffering. Of course some deontologists might claim that though it is logically possible that their principles might conflict with the utilitarian one, *in fact* such a conflict would never occur. It seems that if such a deontology did exist, the utilitarian need not be concerned to defend himself against it, since its practical consequences would not differ from those of utilitarianism. However all deontological systems which are known to me do seem to differ from utilitarianism not only in theory but also in practice.

Such a 'persuasive' objection to deontology is possible simply *because* we have assumed the truth of non-cognitivist (or possibly, subjectivist) meta-ethics. A cognitivist in meta-ethics of the type of Sir David Ross[1] could resist any such appeal to the heart by saying that whether we like it or not his deontological principles can be *seen* to be true. That they might sometimes conflict with human happiness or welfare might seem to him to be more of sentimental than of philosophic concern. But if we strip off the cognitivist meta-ethics from Ross's theory, then his deontology may come to look artificial and perhaps infected by a sort of 'rule worship'. For example the obligation to keep promises seems to be too artificial, to smack too much of human social conventions, to do duty as an ultimate principle. On the other hand it is, as we shall see, harder to produce persuasive arguments against a restrained deontology which supplements the utilitarian principle by principles related to abstract justice and fair distribution. However, I am not attempting

[1] Sir David Ross, *Foundations of Ethics* (Oxford University Press, London, 1939).

to show that the utilitarian can have no philosophically clear-headed rivals, but am merely trying to suggest that it is harder than is commonly believed to produce clear-headed and acceptable deontological systems of ethics, and that the range of these is probably not so wide as to embrace some of the well-known ones, such as that of Sir David Ross.

In setting up a system of normative ethics the utilitarian must appeal to some ultimate attitudes which he holds in common with those people to whom he is addressing himself. The sentiment to which he appeals is generalized benevolence, that is, the disposition to seek happiness, or at any rate, in some sense or other, good consequences, for all mankind, or perhaps for all sentient beings. His audience may not initially be in agreement with the utilitarian position. For example, they may have a propensity to obey the rules of some traditional moral system into which they have been indoctrinated in youth. Nevertheless the utilitarian will have some hope of persuading the audience to agree with his system of normative ethics. As a utilitarian he can appeal to the sentiment of generalized benevolence, which is surely present in any group with whom it is profitable to discuss ethical questions. He may be able to convince some people that their previous disposition to accept non-utilitarian principles was due to conceptual confusions. He will not be able to convince everybody, no doubt, but that utilitarianism will not be accepted by everybody, or even by all philosophically clear-headed people, is not in itself an objection to it. It may well be that there is no ethical system which appeals to all people, or even to the same person in different moods. I shall revert to this matter later on.[1]

To some extent then, I shall be trying to present Sidgwick in a modern dress. The axioms of utilitarianism are no longer the deliverances of intellectual intuition but the expressions

[1] See pp. 72-3 below.

of our ultimate attitudes or feelings. Deductions from these axioms nevertheless go through in very much the same way. In a discussion note commenting on the earlier edition of this monograph, Charles Landesman suggested[1] that as a non-cognitivist I am not entitled to talk about the logical consequences of ethical principles. However it is not clear to me that this is an insuperable difficulty. For example, R. M. Hare[2] and others have worked out theories of logical relations between imperative sentences, and even mere expressions of attitude can be said to be consistent or inconsistent with one another.

Thus 'Boo to snakes' is consistent with 'Boo to reptiles' and inconsistent with 'Hurrah for reptiles'. Indeed there is no reason why a non-cognitivist should refuse to call ethical sentences 'true' or 'false'. He can say '"Smith is good" is true if and only if Smith is good.' He can even say things like 'Some of Buddha's ethical sayings are true', thus giving to understand that he would be in agreement with some of the attitudes expressed in Buddha's sayings, even though he is not telling, and even may not know, which ones these are. I must concede, however, that there are difficulties (attested to by the word 'would' in the previous sentence) in giving a proper semantics on these lines. The semantics for 'would' gets us into talk about possible worlds, which are dubious entities. Again consider a sentence like 'If it rains Smith's action is right.' A non-cognitivist would perhaps interpret this as expressing approval of Smith's action in a possible world in which it is raining. However ethics, whether non-cognitivist or not, probably needs the notion of a possible world,[3] dubious or not, since it is concerned with alternative possible actions, and so in this respect the non-cognitivist

[1] 'A note on act utilitarianism', *Philosophical Review* 73 (1964) 243–7.
[2] *The Language of Morals*.
[3] See R. Montague, 'Logical necessity, physical necessity, ethics, and quantifiers', *Inquiry* 3 (1959) 259–63.

may not really be worse off than the cognitivist. At any rate, I am assuming in this monograph that adequate non-cognitivist theories of meta-ethics exist.

2. Act-utilitarianism and rule-utilitarianism

The system of normative ethics which I am here concerned to defend is, as I have said earlier, *act*-utilitarianism. Act-utilitarianism is to be contrasted with rule-utilitarianism. Act-utilitarianism is the view that the rightness or wrongness of an action is to be judged by the consequences, good or bad, of the action itself. Rule-utilitarianism is the view that the rightness or wrongness of an action is to be judged by the goodness and badness of the consequences of a rule that everyone should perform the action in like circumstances. There are two sub-varieties of rule-utilitarianism according to whether one construes 'rule' here as 'actual rule' or 'possible rule'. With the former, one gets a view like that of S. E. Toulmin[1] and with the latter, one like Kant's.[2] That is, if it is permissible to interpret Kant's principle 'Act only on that maxim through which you can at the same time will that it should become a universal law' as 'Act only on that maxim which you as a humane and benevolent person would like to see established as a universal law.' Of course Kant would resist this appeal to human feeling, but it seems necessary in order to interpret his doctrine in a plausible way. A subtle version of the Kantian type of rule-utilitarianism is given by R. F. Harrod in his 'Utilitarianism Revised'.[3]

---

[1] *An Examination of the Place of Reason in Ethics* (Cambridge University Press, London, 1950).

[2] Immanuel Kant, *Groundwork of the Metaphysic of Morals*. Translated from the German in *The Moral Law*, by H. J. Paton (Hutchinson, London, 1948).

[3] *Mind* 45 (1936) 137–56.

I have argued elsewhere[1] the objections to rule-utilitarianism as compared with act-utilitarianism.[2] Briefly they boil down to the accusation of rule worship:[3] the rule-utilitarian presumably advocates his principle because he is ultimately concerned with human happiness: why then should he advocate abiding by a rule when he knows that it will not in the present case be most beneficial to abide by it? The reply that in most cases it is most beneficial to abide by the rule seems irrelevant. And so is the reply that it would be better that everybody should abide by the rule than that nobody should. This is to suppose that the only alternative to 'everybody does *A*' is 'no one does *A*'. But clearly we have the possibility 'some people do *A* and some don't'. Hence to refuse to break a generally beneficial rule in those cases in which it is not most beneficial to obey it seems irrational and to be a case of rule worship.

The type of utilitarianism which I shall advocate will, then, be act-utilitarianism, not rule-utilitarianism.

David Lyons has recently argued that rule-utilitarianism (by which, I think, he means the sort of rule-utilitarianism which I have called the Kantian one) collapses into act-utilitarianism.[4] His reasons are briefly as follows. Suppose

---

[1] In my article 'Extreme and restricted utilitarianism', *Philosophical Quarterly* 6 (1956) 344–54. This contains bad errors and a better version of the article will be found in Philippa Foot (ed.), *Theories of Ethics* (Oxford University Press, London, 1967), or Michael D. Bayles (ed.), *Contemporary Utilitarianism* (Doubleday, New York, 1968). In this article I used the terms 'extreme' and 'restricted' instead of Brandt's more felicitous 'act' and 'rule'. which I now prefer.

[2] For another discussion of what in effect is the same problem see A. K. Stout's excellent paper, 'But suppose everyone did the same', *Australasian Journal of Philosophy* 32 (1954) 1–29.

[3] On rule worship see I. M. Crombie, 'Social clockwork and utilitarian morality', in D. M. Mackinnon (ed.), *Christian Faith and Communist Faith* (Macmillan, London, 1953). See p. 109.

[4] David Lyons, *The Forms and Limits of Utilitarianism* (Oxford University Press, London, 1965). Rather similar considerations have been put

that an exception to a rule *R* produces the best possible consequences. Then this is evidence that the rule *R* should be modified so as to allow this exception. Thus we get a new rule of the form 'do *R* except in circumstances of the sort *C*'. That is, whatever would lead the act-utilitarian to break a rule would lead the Kantian rule-utilitarian to modify the rule. Thus an adequate rule-utilitarianism would be extensionally equivalent to act-utilitarianism.

Lyons is particularly interested in what he calls 'threshold effects'. A difficulty for rule-utilitarianism has often appeared to be that of rules like 'do not walk on the grass' or 'do not fail to vote at an election'. In these cases it would seem that it is beneficial if some people, though not too many, break the rule. Lyons points out that we can distinguish the action of doing something (say, walking on the grass) after some largish number *n* other people have done it from the action of doing it when few or no people have done it. When these extra circumstances are written into the rule, Lyons holds that the rule will come to enjoin the same actions as would the act-utilitarian principle. However there seems to be one interesting sort of case which requires slightly different treatment. This is the sort of case in which not too many people must do action *X*, but each person must plan his action in ignorance of what the other person does. That is, what *A* does depends on what *B* does, and what *B* does depends on what *A* does. Situations possessing this sort of circularity will be discussed below, pp. 57–62.

I am inclined to think that an adequate rule-utilitarianism would not only be extensionally equivalent to the act-utilitarian principle (i.e. would enjoin the same set of actions

forward by R. M. Hare, *Freedom and Reason* (Oxford University Press, London, 1963), pp. 131–6, and R. B. Brandt, 'Toward a credible from of utilitarianism', in H. N. Castañeda and G. Nakhnikian, *Morality and the Language of Conduct* (Wayne State University Press, Detroit, 1963), esp. pp. 119–23.

as it) but would in fact consist of one rule only, the act-utilitarian one: 'maximize probable benefit'. This is because any rule which can be formulated must be able to deal with an indefinite number of unforeseen types of contingency. No rule, short of the act-utilitarian one, can therefore be safely regarded as extensionally equivalent to the act-utilitarian principle unless it is that very principle itself. I therefore suggest that Lyons' type of consideration can be taken even further, and that rule-utilitarianism of the Kantian sort must collapse into act-utilitarianism in an even stronger way: it must become a 'one-rule' rule-utilitarianism which is identical to act-utilitarianism. In any case, whether this is correct or not, it is with the defence of act-utilitarianism, and not with rule-utilitarianism (supposing that there are viable forms of rule-utilitarianism which may be distinguished from act-utilitarianism) that this monograph is concerned. (Lyons himself rejects utilitarianism.)

3. Hedonistic and non-hedonistic utilitarianism

An act-utilitarian judges the rightness or wrongness of actions by the goodness and badness of their consequences. But is he to judge the goodness and badness of the consequences of an action solely by their pleasantness and un-pleasantness? Bentham,[1] who thought that quantity of pleasure being equal, the experience of playing pushpin was as good as that of reading poetry, could be classified as a hedonistic act-utilitarian. Moore,[2] who believed that some

---

[1] Jeremy Bentham's most important ethical work is 'An Introduction to the Principles of Morals and Legislation', in *A Fragment on Government and an Introduction to the Principles of Morals and Legislation*, ed. Wilfrid Harrison (Blackwell, Oxford, 1948). For the remark on poetry and pushpin see Bentham's *Works* (Tait, Edinburgh, 1843), vol. 2, pp. 253–4.

[2] G. E. Moore, *Principia Ethica* (Cambridge University Press, London, 1962).

states of mind, such as those of acquiring knowledge, had intrinsic value quite independent of their pleasantness, can be called an ideal utilitarian. Mill seemed to occupy an intermediate position.[3] He held that there are higher and lower pleasures. This seems to imply that pleasure is a necessary condition for goodness but that goodness depends on other qualities of experience than pleasantness and unpleasantness. I propose to call Mill a quasi-ideal utilitarian. For Mill, pleasantness functions like x in the algebraic product, $x \times y \times z$. If $x = 0$ the product is zero. For Moore pleasantness functions more like x in $(x + 1) \times y \times z$. If $x = 0$ the product need not be zero. Of course this is only a very rough analogy.

What Bentham, Mill and Moore are all agreed on is that the rightness of an action is to be judged solely by consequences, states of affairs brought about by the action. Of course we shall have to be careful here not to construe 'state of affairs' so widely that any ethical doctrine becomes utilitarian. For if we did so we would not be saying anything at all in advocating utilitarianism. If, for example, we allowed 'the state of having just kept a promise', then a deontologist who said we should keep promises simply because they are promises would be a utilitarian. And we do not wish to allow this.

According to the type of non-cognitivist (or subjectivist) ethics that I am assuming, the function of the words 'ought' and 'good' is primarily to express approval, or in other words, to commend. With 'ought' we commend actions. With 'good' we may commend all sorts of things, but here I am concerned with 'good' as used to commend states of affairs or consequences of actions. Suppose we could know with certainty the total consequences of two alternative actions A and B, and suppose that A and B are the only possible actions open to us. Then in deciding whether we

[3] J. S. Mill, *Utilitarianism*, ed. Mary Warnock (Collins, London, 1962).

ought to do *A* or *B*, the act-utilitarian would ask whether the total consequences of *A* are better than those of *B*, or vice versa, or whether the total consequences are equal. That is, he commends *A* rather than *B* if he thinks that the total consequences of *A* are better than those of *B*. But to say 'better' is itself to commend. So the act-utilitarian has to do a double evaluation or piece of commending. First of all he has to evaluate consequences. Then on the basis of his evaluation of consequences he has to evaluate the actions *A* and *B* which would lead to these two sets of consequences. It is easy to fail to notice that this second evaluation is needed, but we can see that it is necessary if we remind ourselves of the following fact. This is that a non-utilitarian, say a philosopher of the type of Sir David Ross, might agree with us in the evaluation of the relative merits of the total sets of consequences of the actions *A* and *B* and yet disagree with us about whether we ought to do *A* or *B*. He might agree with us in the evaluation of total consequences but disagree with us in the evaluation of possible actions. He might say: "The total consequences of *A* are better than the total consequences of *B*, but it would be *unjust* to do *A*, for you *promised* to do *B*."

My chief concern in this study is with the *second* type of evaluation: the evaluation of actions. The utilitarian addresses himself to people who very likely agree with him as to what consequences are good ones, but who disagree with him about the principle that what we ought to do is to produce the best consequences. For a reason, which will appear presently, the difference between ideal and hedonistic utilitarianism in most cases will not usually lead to a serious disagreement about what ought to be done in practice. In this section, however, I wish to clear the ground by saying something about the *first* type of evaluation, the evaluation of consequences. It is with respect to this evaluation that Bentham, Mill and Moore differ from one another.

Let us consider Mill's contention that it is 'better to be Socrates dissatisfied than a fool satisfied'.[1] Mill holds that pleasure is not to be our sole criterion for evaluating consequences: the state of mind of Socrates might be less pleasurable than that of the fool, but, according to Mill, Socrates would be happier than the fool.

It is necessary to observe, first of all, that a purely hedonistic utilitarian, like Bentham, might agree with Mill in preferring the experiences of discontented philosophers to those of contented fools. His preference for the philosopher's state of mind, however, would not be an *intrinsic* one. He would say that the discontented philosopher is a useful agent in society and that the existence of Socrates is responsible for an improvement in the lot of humanity generally. Consider two brothers. One may be of a docile and easy temperament: he may lead a supremely contented and unambitious life, enjoying himself hugely. The other brother may be ambitious, may stretch his talents to the full, may strive for scientific success and academic honours, and may discover some invention or some remedy for disease or improvement in agriculture which will enable innumerable men of easy temperament to lead a contented life, whereas otherwise they would have been thwarted by poverty, disease or hunger. Or he may make some advance in pure science which will later have beneficial practical applications. Or, again, he may write poetry which will solace the leisure hours and stimulate the brains of practical men or scientists, thus indirectly leading to an improvement in society. That is, the pleasures of poetry or mathematics may be *extrinsically* valuable in a way in which those of pushpin or sun-bathing may not be. Though the poet or

---

[1] *Utilitarianism*, p. 9. The problem of the unhappy sage and the happy fool is cleverly stated in Voltaire's 'Histoire d'un bon Bramin', *Choix de Contes*, edited with an introduction and notes by F. C. Green (Cambridge University Press, London, 1951), pp. 245–7.

mathematician may be discontented, society as a whole may be the more contented for his presence.

Again, a man who enjoys pushpin is likely eventually to become bored with it, whereas the man who enjoys poetry is likely to retain this interest throughout his life. Moreover the reading of poetry may develop imagination and sensitivity, and so as a result of his interest in poetry a man may be able to do more for the happiness of others than if he had played pushpin and let his brain deteriorate. In short, both for the man immediately concerned and for others, the pleasures of poetry are, to use Bentham's word, more *fecund* than those of pushpin.

Perhaps, then, our preference for poetry over pushpin is not one of intrinsic value, but is merely one of extrinsic value. Perhaps strictly in itself and at a particular moment, a contented sheep is as good as a contented philosopher. However it is hard to agree to this. If we did we should have to agree that the human population ought ideally to be reduced by contraceptive methods and the sheep population more than correspondingly increased. Perhaps just so many humans should be left as could keep innumerable millions of placid sheep in contented idleness and immunity from depredations by ferocious animals. Indeed if a contented idiot is as good as a contented philosopher, and if a contented sheep is as good as a contented idiot, then a contented fish is as good as a contented sheep, and a contented beetle is as good as a contented fish. Where shall we stop?

Maybe we have gone wrong in talking of pleasure as though it were no more than contentment. Contentment consists roughly in relative absence of unsatisfied desires; pleasure is perhaps something more positive and consists in a balance between absence of unsatisfied desires and presence of satisfied desires. We might put the difference in this way: pure unconsciousness would be a limiting case of contentment, but not of pleasure. A stone has no unsatisfied desires, but then it just has no desires. Nevertheless, this consideration will not resolve the disagreement between Bentham and Mill. No doubt a dog has as intense a desire to discover rats as the philosopher has to discover the mysteries of the universe. Mill would wish to say that the pleasures of the philosopher were more valuable intrinsically than those of the dog, however intense these last might be.

It appears, then, that many of us may well have a preference not only for enjoyment as such but for certain sorts of enjoyment. And this goes for many of the humane and beneficent readers whom I am addressing. I suspect that they too have an intrinsic preference for the more complex and intellectual pleasures. This is not surprising. We must not underrate the mere brute strength of a hard and fit human being: by any standards man is a large and strong animal. Nevertheless above all else man owes his survival to his superior intelligence. If man were not a species which was inclined above all else to think and strive, we should not be where we are now. No wonder that men have a liking for intelligence and complexity, and this may become increasingly so in future. Perhaps some people may feel that my remarks here are somewhat too complacent, in view of the liking of so many people for low-grade entertainments, such as certain popular television programmes. But even the most avid television addict probably enjoys solving practical problems connected with his car, his furniture, or his garden. However unintellectual he might be, he would certainly resent the suggestion that he should, if it were possible, change places with a contented sheep, or even a lively and happy dog. Nevertheless, when all is said and done, we must not disguise the fact that disagreements in ultimate attitude are possible between those who like Mill have, and those who like Bentham have not, an intrinsic preference for the 'higher' pleasures. However it is possible for two people to disagree about ultimate ends and yet agree in practice about what ought to be done. It is worth while enquiring how much practical ethics is likely to be affected by the possibility of disagreement over the question of Socrates dissatisfied versus the fool satisfied.

'Not very much', one feels like saying at first. We noted that the most complex and intellectual pleasures are also the most fecund. Poetry elevates the mind, makes one more sensitive, and so harmonizes with various intellectual pursuits, some of which are of practical value. Delight in mathematics is even more obviously, on Benthamite views, a pleasure worth encouraging, for on the progress of mathematics depends the progress of mankind. Even the most hedonistic schoolmaster would prefer to see his boys enjoying poetry and mathematics rather than neglecting these arts for the pleasures of marbles or the tuckshop. Indeed many of the brutish pleasures not only lack fecundity but are actually the reverse of fecund. To enjoy food too much is to end up fat, unhealthy and without zest or vigour. To enjoy drink too much is even worse. In most circumstances of ordinary life the pure hedonist will agree in his practical recommendations with the quasi-ideal utilitarian.

This need not always be so. Some years ago two psychologists, Olds and Milner, carried out some experiments with rats.[1] Through the skull of each rat they inserted an electrode. These electrodes penetrated to various regions of the brain. In the case of some of these regions the rat showed

[1] James Olds and Peter Milner, 'Positive reinforcement produced by electrical stimulation of the septal area and other regions of the rat brain', *Journal of Comparative and Physiological Psychology* 47 (1954) 419–27. James Olds, 'A preliminary mapping of electrical reinforcing effect in the rat brain', *ibid.* 49 (1956) 281–5. I. J. Good has also used these results of Olds and Milner in order to discuss ethical hedonism. See his 'A problem for the hedonist', in I. J. Good (ed.), *The Scientist Speculates* (Heinemann London, 1962). Good takes the possibility of this sort of thing to provide a *reductio ad absurdum* of hedonism.

behaviour characteristics of pleasure when a current was passed from the electrode, in others they seemed to show pain, and in others the stimulus seemed neutral. That a stimulus was pleasure-giving was shown by the fact that the rat would learn to pass the current himself by pressing a lever. He would neglect food and make straight for this lever and start stimulating himself. In some cases he would sit there pressing the lever every few seconds for hours on end. This calls up a pleasant picture of the voluptuary of the future, a bald-headed man with a number of electrodes protruding from his skull, one to give the physical pleasure of sex, one for that of eating, one for that of drinking, and so on. Now is this the sort of life that all our ethical planning should culminate in? A few hours' work a week, automatic factories, comfort and security from disease, and hours spent at a switch, continually electrifying various regions of one's brain? Surely not. Men were made for higher things, one can't help wanting to say, even though one knows that men weren't made for anything, but are the product of evolution by natural selection.

It might be said that the objection to continual sensual stimulation of the above sort is that though it would be pleasant in itself it would be infecund of future pleasures. This is often so with the ordinary sensual pleasures. Excessive indulgence in the physical pleasures of sex may possibly have a debilitating effect and may perhaps interfere with the deeper feelings of romantic love. But whether stimulation by the electrode method would have this weakening effect and whether it would impair the possibility of future pleasures of the same sort is another matter. For example, there would be no excessive secretion of hormones. The whole biochemical mechanism would, almost literally, be short-circuited. Maybe, however, a person who stimulated himself by the electrode method would find it so enjoyable that he would neglect all other pursuits. Maybe if everyone became an electrode operator people would lose interest in everything else and the human race would die out.

Suppose, however, that the facts turned out otherwise: that a man could (and would) do his full share of work in the office or the factory and come back in the evening to a few hours contented electrode work, without bad aftereffects. This would be his greatest pleasure, and the pleasure would be so great intrinsically and so easily repeatable that its lack of fecundity would not matter. Indeed perhaps by this time human arts, such as medicine, engineering, agriculture and architecture will have been brought to a pitch of perfection sufficient to enable most of the human race to spend most of its time electrode operating, without compensating pains of starvation, disease and squalor. Would this be a satisfactory state of society? Would this be the millennium towards which we have been striving? Surely the pure hedonist would have to say that it was.

It is time, therefore, that we had another look at the concept of happiness. Should we say that the electrode operator was really happy? This is a difficult question to be clear about, because the concept of happiness is a tricky one. But whether we should call the electrode operator 'happy' or not, there is no doubt (a) that he would be *contented* and (b) that he would be *enjoying himself*.

Perhaps a possible reluctance to call the electrode operator 'happy' might come from the following circumstance. The electrode operator might be perfectly contented, might perfectly enjoy his electrode operating, and might not be willing to exchange his lot for any other. And we ourselves, perhaps, once we became electrode operators too, could become perfectly contented and satisfied. But nevertheless, as we are now, we just do not want to become electrode operators. We want other things, perhaps to write a book or get into a cricket team. If someone said 'from tomorrow onwards you are going to be forced to be an electrode operator' we should not be pleased. Maybe from tomorrow onwards, once the electrode work had started, we should be perfectly contented, but we are not contented now at the prospect. We are not satisfied at being told that we would be in a certain state from tomorrow onwards, even though we may know that from tomorrow onwards we should be perfectly satisfied. All this is psychologically possible. It is just the obverse of a situation which we often find. I remember an occasion on which I was suspended by cable car half-way up a precipitous mountain. As the cable car creaked upwards, apparently so flimsily held above the yawning chasm below, I fervently wished that I had never come in it. When I bought the ticket for the cable car I knew that I should shortly be wishing that I had never bought it. And yet I should have been annoyed if I had been refused it. Again, a man may be very anxious to catch a bus, so as to be in time for a dental appointment, and yet a few minutes later, while the drill is boring into his tooth, may wish that he had missed that bus. It is, contrariwise, perfectly possible that I should be annoyed today if told that from tomorrow onwards I should be an electrode addict, even though I knew that from tomorrow onwards I should be perfectly contented.

This, I think, explains part of our hesitancy about whether to call the electrode operator 'happy'. The notion of happiness ties up with that of contentment: to be fairly happy at least involves being fairly contented, though it involves something more as well. Though we should be contented when we became electrode operators, we are not contented now with the prospect that we should become electrode operators. Similarly if Socrates had become a fool he might thereafter have been perfectly contented. Nevertheless if beforehand he had been told that he would in the future become a fool he would have been even more dissatisfied than in fact he was. This is part of the trouble about the dispute between Bentham and Mill. The case involves the possibility of (a) our being contented if we are in a certain state, and (b) our being contented at the prospect of being so contented. Normally situations in which we should be contented go along with our being contented at the prospect of our getting into such situations. In the case of the electrode operator and in that of Socrates and the fool we are pulled two ways at once.

Now to call a person 'happy' is to say more than that he is contented for most of the time, or even that he frequently enjoys himself and is rarely discontented or in pain. It is, I think, in part to express a favourable attitude to the idea of such a form of contentment and enjoyment. That is, for A to call B 'happy', A must be contented at the prospect of B being in his present state of mind and at the prospect of A himself, should the opportunity arise, enjoying that sort of state of mind. That is, 'happy' is a word which is mainly descriptive (tied to the concepts of contentment and enjoyment) but which is also partly evaluative. It is because Mill approves of the 'higher' pleasures, e.g. intellectual pleasures, so much more than he approves of the more simple and brutish pleasures, that, quite apart from consequences and side effects, he can pronounce the man who enjoys the pleasures of philosophical discourse as 'more happy' than the man who gets enjoyment from pushpin or beer drinking.

The word 'happy' is not wholly evaluative, for there would be something absurd, as opposed to merely unusual, in calling a man who was in pain, or who was not enjoying himself, or who hardly ever enjoyed himself, or who was in a more or less permanent state of intense dissatisfaction, a 'happy' man. For a man to be happy he must, as a minimal condition, be fairly contented and moderately enjoying himself for much of the time. Once this minimal condition is satisfied we can go on to evaluate various types of contentment and enjoyment and to grade them in terms of happiness. Happiness is, of course, a long-term concept in a way that enjoyment is not. We can talk of a man enjoying himself at a quarter past two precisely, but hardly of a man being happy at a quarter past two precisely. Similarly we can talk of it raining at a quarter past two precisely, but hardly about it being a wet climate at a quarter past two precisely. But happiness involves enjoyment at various times, just as a wet climate involves rain at various times.

To be enjoying oneself, Ryle once suggested, is to be doing what you want to be doing and not to be wanting to do anything else,[1] or, more accurately, we might say that one enjoys oneself the more one wants to be doing what one is in fact doing and the less one wants to be doing anything else. A man will not enjoy a round of golf if (a) he does not particularly want to play golf, or (b) though he wants to play golf there is something else he wishes he were doing at the same time, such as buying the vegetables for his wife, filling in his income tax forms, or listening to a lecture on philosophy. Even sensual pleasures come under the same description. For example the pleasure of eating an ice-cream involves having a certain physical sensation, in a way in which the pleasure of golf or of symbolic logic does not, but the man who is enjoying an ice-cream can still be said to be doing what he wants to do (have a certain physical sensation) and not to be wanting to do anything else. If his mind is preoccupied with work or if he is conscious of a pressing engagement somewhere else, he will not enjoy the physical sensation, however intense it be, or will not enjoy it very much.

The hedonistic ideal would then appear to reduce to a state of affairs in which each person is enjoying himself. Since, as we noted, a dog may, as far as we can tell, enjoy chasing a rat as much as a philosopher or a mathematician

[1] Gilbert Ryle, *The Concept of Mind* (Hutchison, London, 1949), p. 108.

may enjoy solving a problem, we must, if we adopt the purely hedonistic position, defend the higher pleasures on account of their fecundity. And that might not turn out to be a workable defence in a world made safe for electrode operators.

To sum up so far, happiness is partly an evaluative concept, and so the utilitarian maxim 'You ought to maximize happiness' is doubly evaluative. There is the possibility of an ultimate disagreement between two utilitarians who differ over the question of pushpin versus poetry, or Socrates dissatisfied versus the fool satisfied. The case of the electrode operator shows that two utilitarians might come to advocate very different courses of actions if they differed about what constituted happiness, and this difference between them would be simply an ultimate difference in attitude. Some other possibilities of the 'science fiction' type will be mentioned briefly on pp. 66-7 below. So I do not wish to say that the difference in ultimate valuation between a hedonistic and a non-hedonistic utilitarian will *never* lead to difference in practice.

Leaving these more remote possibilities out of account, however, and considering the decisions we have to make at present, the question of whether the 'higher' pleasures should be preferred to the 'lower' ones does seem to be of slight practical importance. There are already perfectly good hedonistic arguments for poetry as against pushpin. As has been pointed out, the more complex pleasures are incomparably more fecund than the less complex ones: not only are they enjoyable in themselves but they are a means to further enjoyment. Still less, on the whole, do they lead to disillusionment, physical deterioration or social disharmony. The connoisseur of poetry may enjoy himself no more than the connoisseur of whisky, but he runs no danger of a headache on the following morning. Moreover the question of whether the general happiness would be increased by replacing most of the human population by a bigger population of contented sheep and pigs is not one which by any stretch of the imagination could become a live issue. Even if we thought, on abstract grounds, that such a replacement would be desirable, we should not have the slightest chance of having our ideas generally adopted.

So much for the issue between Bentham and Mill. What about that between Mill and Moore? Could a pleasurable state of mind have no intrinsic value at all, or perhaps even a *negative* intrinsic value?[1] Are there pleasurable states of mind towards which we have an unfavourable attitude, even though we disregard their consequences? In order to decide this question let us imagine a universe consisting of one sentient being only, who falsely believes that there are other sentient beings and that they are undergoing exquisite torment. So far from being distressed by the thought, he takes a great delight in these imagined sufferings. Is this better or worse than a universe containing no sentient being at all? Is it worse, again, than a universe containing only one sentient being with the same beliefs as before but who sorrows at the imagined tortures of his fellow creatures? I suggest, as against Moore, that the universe containing the deluded sadist is the preferable one. After all he is happy, and since there is no other sentient being, what harm can he do? Moore would nevertheless agree that the sadist was happy, and this shows how happiness, though partly an evaluative concept, is also partly not an evaluative concept.

It is difficult, I admit, not to feel an immediate repugnance at the thought of the deluded sadist. If throughout our childhood we have been given an electric shock whenever we had tasted cheese, then cheese would have become immediately distasteful to us. Our repugnance to the sadist arises, naturally enough, because in our universe sadists invariably do harm. If we lived in a universe in which by

[1] Cf. G. E. Moore, *Principia Ethica*, pp. 209–10.

some extraordinary laws of psychology a sadist was always confounded by his own knavish tricks and invariably did a great deal of good, then we should feel better disposed towards the sadistic mentality. Even if we could de-condition ourselves from feeling an immediate repugnance to a sadist (as we could de-condition ourselves from a repugnance to cheese by going through a course in which the taste of cheese was invariably associated with a pleasurable stimulus) language might make it difficult for us to distinguish an extrinsic distaste for sadism, founded on our distaste for the consequences of sadism, from an immediate distaste for sadism as such. Normally when we call a thing 'bad' we mean indifferently to express a dislike for it in itself or to express a dislike for what it leads to. When a state of mind is sometimes extrinsically good and sometimes extrinsically bad, we find it easy to distinguish between our intrinsic and extrinsic preferences for instances of it, but when a state of mind is always, or almost always, extrinsically bad, it is easy for us to confuse an extrinsic distaste for it with an intrinsic one. If we allow for this, it does not seem so absurd to hold that there are no pleasures which are intrinsically bad. Pleasures are bad only because they cause harm to the person who has them or to other people. But if anyone likes to disagree with me about this I do not feel very moved to argue the point. Such a disagreement about ultimate ends is not likely to lead to any disagreement in practice. For in all actual cases there are sufficient extrinsic reasons for abhorring sadism and similar states of mind. *Approximate* agreement about ultimate ends is often quite enough for rational and co-operative moral discourse. In practical cases the possibility of factual disagreement about what causes produce what effects is likely to be overwhelmingly more important than disagreement in ultimate ends between hedonistic and ideal utilitarians.

There are of course many valuations other than that of

the intrinsic goodness of sadistic pleasures which divide the ideal from the hedonistic utilitarian. For example the ideal utilitarian would hold that an intellectual experience, even though not pleasurable, would be intrinsically good. Once more, however, I think we can convince ourselves that in most cases this disagreement about ends will not lead to disagreement about means. Intellectual experiences are in the hedonistic view extrinsically good. Of course there may be wider issues dividing the hedonistic from the ideal utilitarian, if Moore is the ideal utilitarian. I would argue that Moore's principle of organic unities destroys the essential utilitarianism of his doctrine. He need never disagree in practice as a utilitarian ought to, with Sir David Ross. Every trick that Ross can play with his *prima facie* duties, Moore can play, in a different way, with his organic unities.[1]

4. Average happiness versus total happiness

Another type of ultimate disagreement between utilitarians, whether hedonistic or ideal, can arise over whether we should try to maximize the *average* happiness of human beings (or the average goodness of their states of mind) or whether we should try to maximize the *total* happiness or goodness. (I owe this point to my friend A. G. N. Flew.) I have not yet elucidated the concept of total happiness, and you may regard it as a suspect notion. But for present purposes I shall put it in this way: Would you be quite indifferent between (a) a universe containing only one million happy sentient beings, all equally happy, and (b) a

[1] A similar point is made by A. C. Ewing in his article 'Recent developments in British ethical thought', in C. A. Mace (ed.), *British Philosophy in the Mid-Century* (Allen and Unwin, London, 1957; second edition 1966). Ewing sees it not as I have done as showing that the principle of organic unities destroys the utilitarian character of a theory, but as a way of reconciling utilitarianism with Rossian principles.

universe containing two million happy beings, each neither more nor less happy than any in the first universe? Or would you, as a humane and sympathetic person, give a preference to the second universe? I myself cannot help feeling a preference for the second universe.[1] But if someone feels the other way I do not know how to argue with him. It looks as though we have yet another possibility of disagreement within a general utilitarian framework.

This type of disagreement might have practical relevance. It might be important in discussions of the ethics of birth control. This is not to say that the utilitarian who values total, rather than average, happiness may not have potent arguments in favour of birth control. But he will need more arguments to convince himself than will the other type of utilitarian.

In most cases the difference between the two types of utilitarianism will not lead to disagreement in practice. For in most cases the most effective way to increase the total happiness is to increase the average happiness, and vice versa.

5. Negative utilitarianism

Sir Karl Popper has suggested[2] that we should concern ourselves not so much with the maximization of happiness as with the minimization of suffering. By 'suffering' we must understand misery involving actual pain, not just unhappiness. For otherwise the doctrine becomes unclear. Suppose that we found a new university. We may hope that indirectly research will help to minimize pains, but that is not the only

---

[1] This does not mean that I approve of the present explosive increase in world population. A typical member of an over-populated planet is *not* equally happy with a typical member of a moderately populated planet.

[1] *The Open Society and its Enemies*, 5th ed. (Routledge and Kegan Paul, London, 1966), vol. 1, ch. 5, note 6.

reason why we found universities. We do so partly because we want the happiness of understanding the world. But producing the happiness of understanding could equally well be thought of as removing the unhappiness of ignorance.

Let us see what sort of utilitarian position we should develop if we made the minimization of misery our sole ultimate ethical principle. The doctrine of negative utilitarianism, that we should concern ourselves with the minimization of suffering rather than with the maximization of happiness, does seem to be a theoretically possible one. It does, however, have some very curious consequences, which have been pointed out by my brother, R. N. Smart.[1] In virtue of these very curious consequences I doubt whether negative utilitarianism will commend itself to many people, though it is always possible that someone might feel so attracted by the principle that he would accept it in spite of its consequences. For example it is possible to argue that a negative utilitarian would have to be in favour of exterminating the human race. It seems likely that Popper is himself not a utilitarian, and so *a fortiori* not a negative utilitarian. For alongside the negative utilitarian principle he sets two principles, that we should tolerate the tolerant, and that we should resist tyranny.[2] It is hard to see how these principles could be deduced from the negative utilitarian principle, for surely, as my brother has pointed out, on this principle we should approve of a tyrannical but benevolent world exploder. Such a tyrant would prevent infinite future misery.

Even though we may not be attracted to negative utilitarianism as an ultimate principle, we may concede that the injunction 'worry about removing misery rather than about promoting happiness' has a good deal to recommend

[1] 'Negative utilitarianism', *Mind* 67 (1958) 542–3.
[2] Popper, *The Open Society and its Enemies*.

it as a subordinate rule of thumb. For in most cases we can do most for our fellow men by trying to remove their miseries. Moreover people will be less ready to agree on what goods they would like to see promoted than they will be to agree on what miseries should be avoided. Mill and Bentham might disagree on whether poetry should be preferred to pushpin, but they would agree that an occasional visit to the dentist is preferable to chronic toothache. While there are so many positive evils in the world there is plenty of scope for co-operative effort among men who may nevertheless disagree to some extent as to what constitute positive goods.

6. Rightness and wrongness of actions

I shall now state the act-utilitarian doctrine. Purely for simplicity of exposition I shall put it forward in a broadly hedonistic form. If anyone values states of mind such as knowledge independently of their pleasurableness he can make appropriate verbal alterations to convert it from hedonistic to ideal utilitarianism. And I shall not here take sides on the issue between hedonistic and quasi-ideal utilitarianism. I shall concern myself with the evaluation signified by 'ought' in 'one ought to do that which will produce the best consequences', and leave to one side the evaluation signified by the word 'best'.

Let us say, then, that the only reason for performing an action *A* rather than an alternative action *B* is that doing *A* will make mankind (or, perhaps, all sentient beings) happier than will doing *B*. (Here I put aside the consideration that in fact we can have only probable belief about the effects of our actions, and so our reason should be more precisely stated as that doing *A* will produce more probable benefit than will doing *B*. For convenience of exposition I shelve this question of probability for a page or two.) This is so simple and natural a doctrine that we can surely expect that many of my readers will have at least some propensity to agree. For I am talking, as I said earlier, to sympathetic and benevolent men, that is, to men who desire the happiness of mankind. Since they have a favourable attitude to the general happiness, surely they will have a tendency to submit to an ultimate moral principle which does no more than express this attitude. It is true that these men, being human, will also have purely selfish attitudes. Either these attitudes will be in harmony with the general happiness (in cases where everyone's looking after his own interests promotes the maximum general happiness) or they will not be in harmony with the general happiness, in which case they will largely cancel one another out, and so could not be made the basis of an interpersonal discussion anyway. It is possible, then, that many sympathetic and benevolent people depart from or fail to attain a utilitarian ethical principle only under the stress of tradition, of superstition, or of unsound philo-sophical reasoning. If this hypothesis should turn out to be correct, at least as far as these readers are concerned, then the utilitarian may contend that there is no need for him to defend his position directly, save by stating it in a consistent manner, and by showing that common objections to it are unsound. After all, it expresses an ultimate attitude, not a liking for something merely as a means to something else. Save for attempting to remove confusions and discredit superstitions which may get in the way of clear moral thinking, he cannot, of course, appeal to argument and must rest his hopes on the good feeling of his readers. If any reader is not a sympathetic and benevolent man, then of course it cannot be expected that he will have an ultimate pro-attitude to human happiness in general. Also some good-hearted readers may reject the utilitarian position because of certain considerations relating to justice. I postpone dis-cussion of these until pp. 67–73.

The utilitarian's ultimate moral principle, let it be remembered, expresses the sentiment not of altruism but of benevolence, the agent counting himself neither more nor less than any other person. Pure altruism cannot be made the basis of a universal moral discussion in that it would lead different people to different and perhaps incompatible courses of action, even though the circumstances were identical. When two men each try to let the other through a door first a deadlock results. Altruism could hardly commend itself to those of a scientific, and hence universalistic, frame of mind. If you count in my calculations why should I not count in your calculations? And why should I pay more attention to my calculations than to yours? Of course we often tend to praise and honour altruism even more than generalized benevolence. This is because people too often err on the side of selfishness, and so altruism is a fault on the right side. If we can make a man try to be an altruist he may succeed as far as acquiring a generalized benevolence.

Suppose we could predict the future consequences of actions with certainty. Then it would be possible to say that the total future consequences of action A are such-and-such and that the total future consequences of action B are so-and-so. In order to help someone to decide whether to do A or to do B we could say to him: 'Envisage the total consequences of A, and think them over carefully and imaginatively. Now envisage the total consequences of B, and think them over carefully. As a benevolent and humane man, and thinking of yourself just as one man among others, would you prefer the consequences of A or those of B?' That is, we are asking for a comparison of one (present and future) *total* situation with another (present and future) *total* situation. So far we are not asking for a *summation* or *calculation* of pleasures or happiness. We are asking only for a comparison of total situations. And it seems clear that we can frequently make such a comparison and say that one total situation is better than another. For example few people would not prefer a total situation in which a million people are well-fed, well-clothed, free of pain, doing interesting and enjoyable work, and enjoying the pleasures of conversation, study, business, art, humour, and so on, to a total situation where there are ten thousand such people only, or perhaps 999,999 such people plus one man with toothache, or neurotic, or shivering with cold. In general, we can sum things up by saying that if we are humane, kindly, benevolent people, we want as many people as possible now and in the future to be as happy as possible. Someone might object that we cannot envisage the total future situation, because this stretches into infinity. In reply to this we may say that it does not stretch into infinity, as all sentient life on earth will ultimately be extinguished, and furthermore we do not normally in practice need to consider very remote consequences, as these in the end approximate rapidly to zero like the furthermost ripples on a pond after a stone has been dropped into it.

But do the remote consequences of an action diminish to zero? Suppose that two people decide whether to have a child or remain childless. Let us suppose that they decide to have the child, and that they have a limitless succession of happy descendants. The remote consequences do not seem to get less. Not at any rate if these people are Adam and Eve. The difference would be between the end of the human race and a limitless accretion of human happiness, generation by generation. The Adam and Eve example shows that the 'ripples on the pond' postulate is not needed in every case for a rational utilitarian decision. If we had some reason for thinking that every generation would be more happy than not we would not (in the Adam and Eve sort of case) need to be worried that the remote consequences of our action would be in detail unknown. The necessity for the 'ripples in the pond' postulate comes from the fact that usually we do not know whether remote consequences will be good or bad. Therefore we cannot know what to do unless we can assume that remote consequences can be left out of account. This can often be done. Thus if we consider two actual parents, instead of Adam and Eve, then they need not worry about thousands of years hence. Not, at least, if we assume that there will be ecological forces determining the future population of the world. If these parents do not have remote descendants, then other people will presumably have more than they would otherwise. And there is no reason to suppose that my descendants would be more or less happy than yours. We must note, then, that unless we are dealing with 'all or nothing' situations (such as the Adam and Eve one, or that of someone in a position to end human life altogether) we need some sort of 'ripples in the pond' postulate to make utilitarianism workable in practice. I do not know how to prove such a postulate, though it seems plausible enough. If it is not accepted, not only utilitarianism, but also deontological systems like that of Sir David Ross, who at least admits beneficence as one *prima facie* duty among the others, will be fatally affected.

Sometimes, of course, more needs to be said. For example one course of action may make some people very happy and leave the rest as they are or perhaps slightly less happy. Another course of action may make all men rather more happy than before but no one very happy. Which course of action makes mankind happier on the whole? Again, one course of action may make it highly probable that everyone will be made a little happier whereas another course of action may give us a much smaller probability that everyone will be made very much happier. In the third place, one course of action may make everyone happy in a pig-like way, whereas another course of action may make a few people happy in a highly complex and intellectual way.

It seems therefore that we have to weigh the maximizing of happiness against equitable distribution, to weigh probabilities with happiness, and to weigh the intellectual and other qualities of states of mind with their pleasurableness. Are we not therefore driven back to the necessity of some calculus of happiness? Can we just say: "envisage two total situations and tell me which you prefer"? If this were possible, of course there would be no need to talk of summing happiness or of a calculus. All we should have to do would be to put total situations in an order of preference. Since this is not always possible there is a difficulty, to which I shall return shortly.

We have already considered the question of intellectual versus non-intellectual pleasures and activities. This is irrelevant to the present issue because there seems to be no reason why the ideal or quasi-ideal utilitarian cannot use the method of envisaging total situations just as much as the hedonistic utilitarian. It is just a matter of envisaging various alternative total situations, stretching out into the future, and saying which situation one prefers. The non-hedonistic utilitarian may evaluate the total situations differently from the hedonistic utilitarian, in which case there will be an ultimate ethical disagreement. This possibility of ultimate disagreement is always there, though we have given reasons for suspecting that it will not frequently lead to important disagreement in practice.

Let us now consider the question of equity. Suppose that we have the choice of sending four equally worthy and intelligent boys to a medium-grade public school or of leaving three in an adequate but uninspiring grammar school and sending one to Eton. (For sake of the example I am making the almost certainly incorrect assumption that Etonians are happier than other public-school boys and that these other public-school boys are happier than grammar-school boys.) Which course of action makes the most for the happiness of the four boys? Let us suppose that we can neglect complicating factors, such as that the superior

Etonian education might lead one boy to develop his talents so much that he will have an extraordinary influence on the well-being of mankind, or that the unequal treatment of the boys might cause jealousy and rift in the family. Let us suppose that the Etonian will be as happy as (we may hope) Etonians usually are, and similarly for the other boys, and let us suppose that remote effects can be neglected. Should we prefer the greater happiness of one boy to the moderate happiness of all four? Clearly one parent may prefer one total situation (one boy at Eton and three at the grammar school) while another may prefer the other total situation (all four at the medium-grade public school). Surely both parents have an equal claim to being sympathetic and benevolent, and yet their difference of opinion here is not founded on an empirical disagreement about facts. I suggest, however, that there are not in fact many cases in which such a disagreement could arise. Probably the parent who wished to send one son to Eton would draw the line at sending one son to Eton plus giving him expensive private tuition during the holidays plus giving his other sons no secondary education at all. It is only within rather small limits that this sort of disagreement about equity can arise. Furthermore the cases in which we can make one person *very* much happier without increasing *general* happiness are rare ones. The law of diminishing returns comes in here. So, in most practical cases, a disagreement about what should be done will be an empirical disagreement about what total situation is likely to be brought about by an action, and will not be a disagreement about which total situation is preferable. For example the inequalitarian parent might get the other to agree with him if he could convince him that there was a much higher probability of an Etonian benefiting the human race, such as by inventing a valuable drug or opening up the mineral riches of Antarctica, than there is of a non-Etonian doing so. (Once more I should like to say that I do not myself take such a possibility very seriously!) I must again stress that since disagreement about what causes produce what effects is in practice so much the most important sort of disagreement, to have intelligent moral discussion with a person we do not in fact need complete agreement with him about ultimate ends: an approximate agreement is sufficient.

Rawls[1] has suggested that we must maximize the general happiness only if we do so in a *fair* way. An *unfair* way of maximizing the general happiness would be to do so by a method which involved making some people less happy than they might be otherwise.[2] As against this suggestion a utilitarian might make the following rhetorical objection: if it is rational for me to choose the pain of a visit to the dentist in order to prevent the pain of toothache, why is it not rational of me to choose a pain for Jones, similar to that of my visit to the dentist, if that is the only way in which I can prevent a pain, equal to that of my toothache, for Robinson? Such situations continually occur in war, in mining, and in the fight against disease, when we may often find ourselves in the position of having in the general interest to inflict suffering on good and happy men. However it must be conceded that these objections against fairness as an *ultimate* principle must be rhetorical only, and that Rawls's principle could perhaps be incorporated in a restrained system of deontological ethics, which would avoid the artificiality of the usual forms of deontology. There are in any case plenty of good utilitarian reasons for adopting the principle of fairness as an important, but not inviolable, rule of thumb.

We must now deal with the difficulty about probability. We have so far avoided the common objection to utilitarianism that it involves the allegedly absurd notion of a

[1] 'Justice as fairness', *Philosophical Review* 67 (1958) 164–94.
[2] See especially p. 168 of Rawls's article.

summation or calculus of happiness or goodness. We have done this by using the method of comparing total situations. All we have to do is to envisage two or more total situations and say which we prefer. A purely ordinal, not a quantitative, judgement is all we require. However in taking this position we have oversimplified the matter. Unfortunately we cannot say with certainty what would be the various total situations which could result from our actions. Worse still, we cannot even assign rough probabilities to the total situations as a whole. All we can do is to assign various probabilities to the various possible effects of an action. For example, one course of action may almost certainly lead to a fairly good result next year together with a high probability of a slightly good result the year after, while another action may give a very small probability of a moderately good result the year after and a very small but not negligible probability of a rather bad result the year after that. (I am assuming that in both cases the still more remote results become negligible or such as to cancel one another out.) If we had to weight total situations with probabilities, this would give us enough conceptual difficulty, but it now appears that we have to go within total situations and weight different elements within them according to different probabilities. We seem to be driven back towards a calculus.

If it were possible to assign numerical probabilities to the various effects of our actions we could devise a way of applying the method of total situations. Suppose that we could say that an action X would either give Smith the pleasure of eating ice-cream with probability $4/5$ or the pain of toothache with probability $1/5$ and that it would give Jones the pleasure of sympathy with probability $3/5$ or the displeasure of envy with probability $2/5$ and that no other important results (direct or indirect) would accrue. Suppose that the only alternative action to X is Y and that this has no effect on Smith but causes Jones to go to sleep with probability $3/5$

or to go for a walk with probability 2/5 and that no other important results (direct or indirect) would accrue. Then we could say that the total situations we have to imagine and to compare are (a) (for X): four people (just like Smith) eating ice-cream plus one (just like Smith) with toothache plus three sympathetic people (just like Jones) plus two envious people (just like Jones), and (b) (for Y): three people (just like Jones) who are asleep plus two (just like Jones) going for a walk. In the example I have, for convenience, taken all probabilities to be multiples of 1/5. If they did not have common denominators we should have to make them such, by expressing them as multiples of a denominator which is the lowest common multiple of the original denominators.

However it is not usually possible to assign a numerical probability to a particular event. No doubt we could use actuarial tables to ascertain the probability that a friend of ours, who is of a certain age, a certain carefully specified medical history, and a certain occupation, will die within the next year. But can we give a numerical value to the probability that a new war will break out, that a proof of Fermat's last theorem will be found, or that our knowledge of genetical linkage in human chromosomes will be much improved in the next five years? Surely it is meaningless to talk of a numerical value for these probabilities, and it is probabilities of this sort with which we have to deal in our moral life.

When, however, we look at the way in which in fact we take some of our ordinary practical decisions we see that there is a sense in which most people think that we can weigh up probabilities and advantages. A man deciding whether to migrate to a tropical country may well say to himself, for example, that he can expect a pleasanter life for himself and his family in that country, unless there is a change in the system of government there, which is not very likely, or unless one of his children catches an epidemic disease, which is perhaps rather more likely, and so on, and thinking over all these advantages and disadvantages and probabilities and improbabilities he may come out with the statement that on the whole it seems preferable for him to go there or with the statement that on the whole it seems preferable for him to stay at home.

If we are able to take account of probabilities in our ordinary prudential decisions it seems idle to say that in the field of ethics, the field of our universal and humane attitudes, we cannot do the same thing, but must rely on some dogmatic morality, in short on some set of rules or rigid criteria. Maybe sometimes we just will be unable to say whether we prefer for humanity an improbable great advantage or a probable small advantage, and in these cases perhaps we shall have to toss a penny to decide what to do. Maybe we have not any precise methods for deciding what to do, but then our imprecise methods must just serve their turn. We need not on that account be driven into authoritarianism, dogmatism or romanticism.

So, at any rate, it appears at first sight. But if I cannot say any more the utilitarian position as it is here presented has a serious weakness. The suggested method of developing normative ethics is to appeal to feelings, namely of benevolence, and to reason, in the sense of conceptual clarification and also of empirical enquiry, but not, as so many moralists do, to what the ordinary man says or thinks. The ordinary man is frequently irrational in his moral thinking. And if he can be irrational about morals why cannot he be irrational about probabilities? The fact that the ordinary man thinks that he can weigh up probabilities in making prudential decisions does not mean that there is really any sense in what he is doing. What utilitarianism badly needs, in order to make its theoretical foundations secure, is some method according to which numerical probabilities, even approximate ones, could in theory, though not necessarily always in practice, be assigned to any imagined future event.

D. Davidson and P. Suppes have proposed a method whereby, at any rate in simplified situations, *subjective* probabilities can be given a numerical value.[1] Their theory was to some extent anticipated in an essay by F. P. Ramsey,[2] in which he tries to show how numbers can be assigned to probabilities in the sense of degrees of belief. This allows us to give a theory of rational, in the sense of *self-consistent*, utilitarian choice, but to make utilitarianism thoroughly satisfactory we need something more. We need a method of assigning numbers to *objective*, not subjective, probabilities. Perhaps one method might be to accept the Davidson–Suppes method of assigning subjective probabilities, and define objective probabilities as the subjective probabilities of an unbiased and far-sighted man. This, however, would require independent criteria for lack of bias and for far-sightedness. I do not know how to do this, but I suspect, from the work that is at present being done on decision-making, that the situation may not be hopeless. But until we have an adequate theory of *objective* probability utilitarianism is not on a secure theoretical basis.[3] Nor, for that matter, is ordinary prudence; nor are deontological systems of ethics, like that of Sir David Ross, which assign some weight to beneficence. And any system of deontological ethics implies some method of weighing up the claims of conflicting *prima facie* duties, for it is impossible that deontological rules of conduct should *never* conflict, and the

[1] D. Davidson, P. Suppes, and S. Siegel, *Decision Making: An Experimental Approach* (Stanford University Press, Stanford, California, 1957).

[2] F. P. Ramsey, *The Foundations of Mathematics* (Routledge and Kegan Paul, London, 1931), ch. 7, 'Truth and probability'.

[3] R. McNaughton's interesting article 'A metrical concept of happiness', *Philosophy and Phenomenological Research* 14 (1953–4) 171–83, does not enable us to propose a complete utilitarian calculus, because it neglects probability considerations.

rationale of this is perhaps even more insecure than is the theory of objective probability.

7. The place of rules in act-utilitarianism

According to the act-utilitarian, then, the rational way to decide what to do is to decide to perform that one of those alternative actions open to us (including the null-action, the doing of nothing) which is likely to maximize the probable happiness or well-being of humanity as a whole, or more accurately, of all sentient beings.[1] The utilitarian position is here put forward as a criterion of rational choice. It is true that we may choose to habituate ourselves to behave in accordance with certain rules, such as to keep promises, in the belief that behaving in accordance with these rules is generally optimific, and in the knowledge that we most often just do not have time to work out individual pros and cons. When we act in such an habitual fashion we do not of course deliberate or make a choice. The act-utilitarian will, however, regard these rules as mere rules of thumb, and will use them only as rough guides. Normally he will act in accordance with them when he has no time for considering probable consequences or when the advantages of such a consideration of consequences are likely to be outweighed by the disadvantage of the waste of time involved. He acts in accordance with rules, in short, when there is no time to think, and since he does not think, the

[1] In the first edition of this monograph I said 'which is likely to bring about the total situation now and in the future which is the best for the happiness or well-being of humanity as a whole, or more accurately, of all sentient beings'. This is inaccurate. To probably maximize the benefit is not the same as to maximize the probable benefit. This has been pointed out by David Braybrooke. See p. 35 of his article 'The choice between utilitarianisms', *American Philosophical Quarterly* 4 (1967) 28–38.

actions which he does habitually are not the outcome
of moral thinking. When he has to think what to do,
then there is a question of deliberation or choice, and it is
precisely for such situations that the utilitarian criterion is
intended.

It is, moreover, important to realize that there is no
inconsistency whatever in an act-utilitarian's schooling himself to act, in normal circumstances, habitually and in
accordance with stereotyped rules. He knows that a man
about to save a drowning person has no time to consider
various possibilities, such as that the drowning person is a
dangerous criminal who will cause death and destruction,
or that he is suffering from a painful and incapacitating disease from which death would be a merciful release, or that
various timid people, watching from the bank, will suffer a
heart attack if they see anyone else in the water. No, he
knows that it is almost always right to save a drowning man,
and in he goes. Again, he knows that we would go mad if
we went in detail into the probable consequences of keeping
or not keeping every trivial promise: we will do most good
and reserve our mental energies for more important matters
if we simply habituate ourselves to keep promises in all
normal situations. Moreover he may suspect that on some
occasions personal bias may prevent him from reasoning in a
correct utilitarian fashion. Suppose he is trying to decide
between two jobs, one of which is more highly paid than
the other, though he has given an informal promise that he
will take the lesser paid one. He may well deceive himself
by underestimating the effects of breaking the promise (in
causing loss of confidence) and by overestimating the good
he can do in the highly paid job. He may well feel that if he
trusts to the accepted rules he is more likely to act in the
way that an unbiased act-utilitarian would recommend than
he would be if he tried to evaluate the consequences of
his possible actions himself. Indeed Moore argued on

act-utilitarian grounds that one should never in concrete cases think as an act-utilitarian.[1]

This, however, is surely to exaggerate both the usefulness of rules and the human mind's propensity to unconscious bias. Nevertheless, right or wrong, this attitude of Moore's has a rational basis and (though his argument from probability considerations is faulty in detail) is not the law worship of the rule-utilitarian, who would say that we ought to keep to a rule that is the most generally optimific, even though we *knew* that obeying it in this particular instance would have bad consequences.

Nor is this utilitarian doctrine incompatible, as M. A. Kaplan[2] has suggested it is, with a recognition of the importance of warm and spontaneous expressions of emotion. Consider a case in which a man sees that his wife is tired, and simply from a spontaneous feeling of affection for her he offers to wash the dishes. Does utilitarianism imply that he should have stopped to calculate the various consequences of his different possible courses of action? Certainly not. This would make married life a misery and the utilitarian knows very well as a rule of thumb that on occasions of this sort it is best to act spontaneously and without calculation. Moreover I have said that act-utilitarianism is meant to give a method of deciding what to do in those cases in which we do indeed decide what to do. On these occasions when we do not act as a result of deliberation and choice, that is, when we act spontaneously, no method of decision, whether utilitarian or non-utilitarian, comes into the matter. What

[1] *Principia Ethica,* p. 162.

[2] Morton A. Kaplan, 'Some problems of the extreme utilitarian position', *Ethics* 70 (1959–60) 228–32. This is a critique of my earlier article 'Extreme and restricted utilitarianism', *Philosophical Quarterly* 6 (1956) 344–54. He also puts forward a game theoretic argument against me, but this seems cogent only against an egoistic utilitarian. Kaplan continued the discussion in his interesting note 'Restricted utilitarianism', *Ethics* 71 (1960–1) 301–2.

does arise for the utilitarian is the question of whether or not he should consciously encourage in himself the tendency to certain types of spontaneous feeling. There are in fact very good utilitarian reasons why we should by all means cultivate in ourselves the tendency to certain types of warm and spontaneous feeling.

Though even the act-utilitarian may on occasion act habitually and in accordance with particular rules, his criterion is, as we have said, *applied* in cases in which he does not act habitually but in which he deliberates and chooses what to do. Now the right action for an agent in given circumstances is, we have said, that action which produces better results than any alternative action. If two or more actions produce equally good results, and if these results are better than the results of any other action open to the agent, then there is no such thing as *the* right action: there are two or more actions which are *a* right action. However this is a very exceptional state of affairs, which may well never in fact occur, and so usually I will speak loosely of the action which is *the* right one. We are now able to specify more clearly what is meant by 'alternative action' here. The fact that the utilitarian criterion is meant to apply in situations of deliberation and choice enables us to say that the class of alternative actions which we have in mind when we talk about an action having the best possible results is the class of actions which the agent could have performed if he had tried. For example, it would be better to bring a man back to life than to offer financial assistance to his dependants, but because it is technologically impossible to bring a man back to life, bringing the man back to life is not something we could do if we tried. On the other hand it may well be possible for us to give financial assistance to the dependants, and this then may be the right action. The right action is the action among those which we could do, i.e. those which we *would* do if we chose to, which has the best possible results.

c

It is true that the general concept of action is wider than that of deliberate choice. Many actions are performed habitually and without deliberation. But the actions for whose rightness we as agents want a criterion are, in the nature of the case, those done thinkingly and deliberately. An action is at any rate that sort of human performance which it is appropriate to praise, blame, punish or reward, and since it is often appropriate to praise, blame, punish, or reward habitual performances, the concept of action cannot be identified with that of the outcome of deliberation and choice. With habitual actions the only question that arises for an agent is that of whether or not he should strengthen the habit or break himself of it. And individual acts of habit-strengthening or habit-breaking can themselves be deliberate.

The utilitarian criterion, then, is designed to help a person, who could do various things if he chose to do them, to decide which of these things he should do. His utilitarian deliberation is one of the causal antecedents of his action, and it would be pointless if it were not. The utilitarian view is therefore perfectly compatible with determinism. The only sense of 'he could have done otherwise' that we require is the sense 'he would have done otherwise if he had chosen'. Whether the utilitarian view necessitates complete metaphysical determinism is another matter. All that it requires is that deliberation should determine actions in the way that everyone knows it does anyway. If it is argued that any indeterminism in the universe entails that we can never know the outcome of our actions, we can reply that in normal cases these indeterminacies will be so numerous as approximately to cancel one another out, and anyway all that we require for rational action is that some consequences of our actions should be *more probable* than others, and this is something which no indeterminist is likely to deny.

The utilitarian may now conveniently make a terminological recommendation. Let us use the word 'rational' as a term of commendation for that action which is, on the evidence available to the agent, *likely* to produce the best results, and to reserve the word 'right' as a term of commendation for the action which does *in fact* produce the best results. That is, let us say that what is rational is to try to perform the right action, to try to produce the best results. Or at least this formulation will do where there is an equal probability of achieving each possible set of results. If there is a very low probability of producing very good results, then it is natural to say that the rational agent would perhaps go for other more probable though not quite so good results. For a more accurate formulation we should have to weight the goodness of the results with their probabilities. However, neglecting this complication, we can say, roughly, that it is rational to perform the action which is on the available evidence the one which will produce the best results. This allows us to say, for example, that the agent did the right thing but irrationally (he was trying to do something else, or was trying to do this very thing but went about it unscientifically) and that he acted rationally but by bad luck did the wrong thing, because the things that seemed probable to him, for the best reasons, just did not happen.

Roughly, then: we shall use 'right' and 'wrong' to appraise choices on account of their actual success in promoting the general happiness, and we shall use 'rational' and 'irrational' to appraise them on account of their likely success. As was noted above (p. 42) 'likely success' must be interpreted in terms of maximizing the probable benefit, not in terms of probably maximizing the benefit. In effect, it is rational to do what you reasonably think to be right, and what will be right is what will maximize the probable benefit. We need, however, to make one qualification to this. A person may unreasonably believe what it would in fact be reasonable to believe. We shall still call such a person's action irrational.

If the agent has been unscientific in his calculation of means–ends relationships he may decide that a certain course of action is probably best for human happiness, and it may indeed be so. When he performs this action we may still call his action irrational, because it was pure luck, not sound reasoning, that brought him to his conclusion.

'Rational' and 'irrational' and 'right' and 'wrong' so far have been introduced as terms of appraisal for chosen or deliberate actions only. There is no reason why we should not use the pair of terms 'right' and 'wrong' more widely so as to appraise even habitual actions. Nevertheless we shall not have much occasion to appraise actions that are not the outcome of choice. What we do need is a pair of terms of appraisal for *agents* and *motives*. I suggest that we use the terms 'good' and 'bad' for these purposes. A good agent is one who acts more nearly in a generally optimific way than does the average one. A bad agent is one who acts in a less optimific way than the average. A good motive is one which generally results in beneficent actions, and a bad motive is one which generally ends in maleficent actions. Clearly there is no inconsistency in saying that on a particular occasion a good man did a wrong action, that a bad man did a right action, that a right action was done from a bad motive, or that a wrong action was done from a good motive. Many specious arguments against utilitarianism come from obscuring these distinctions. Thus one may be got to admit that an action is 'right', meaning no more than that it is done from a good motive and is praiseworthy, and then it is pointed out that the action is not 'right' in the sense of being optimific. I do not wish to legislate as to how other people (particularly non-utilitarians) should use words like 'right' and 'wrong', but in the interests of clarity it is important for me to state how I propose to use them myself, and to try to keep the various distinctions clear.

It should be noted that in making this terminological

recommendation I am not trying to smuggle in valuations under the guise of definitions, as Ardon Lyon, in a review of the first edition of this monograph,[1] has suggested that I have done. It is merely a recommendation to pre-empt the already evaluative words 'rational' and 'irrational' for one lot of commendatory or discommendatory jobs, the already evaluative words 'right' and 'wrong' for another lot of commendatory or discommendatory jobs, and the already evaluative words 'good' and 'bad' for yet another lot of commendatory or discommendatory jobs.

We can also use 'good' and 'bad' as terms of commendation or discommendation of actions themselves. In this case to commend or discommend an action is to commend or discommend the motive from which it sprang. This allows us to say that a man performed a bad action but that it was the right one, or that he performed a good action but that it was wrong. For example, a man near Berchtesgaden in 1938 might have jumped into a river and rescued a drowning man, only to find that it was Hitler. He would have done the wrong thing, for he would have saved the world a lot of trouble if he had left Hitler below the surface. On the other hand his motive, the desire to save life, would have been one which we approve of people having: in general, though not in this case, the desire to save life leads to acting rightly. It is worth our while to strengthen such a desire. Not only should we praise the action (thus expressing our approval of it) but we should perhaps even give the man a medal, thus encouraging others to emulate it. Indeed praise itself comes to have some of the social functions of medal giving: we come to like praise for its own sake, and are thus influenced by the possibility of being given it. Praising a person is thus an important action in itself – it has significant effects. A utilitarian must therefore learn to control his acts of praise and dispraise, thus perhaps concealing his approval

[1] *Durham University Journal* 55 (1963) 86–7.

of an action when he thinks that the expression of such approval might have bad effects, and perhaps even praising actions of which he does not really approve. Consider, for example, the case of an act-utilitarian, fighting in a war, who succeeds in capturing the commander of an enemy submarine. Assuming that it is a just war and that the act-utilitarian is fighting on the right side, the very courage and ability of the submarine commander has a tendency which is the reverse of optimific. Everything that the submarine commander has been doing was (in my proposed sense of the word) wrong. (I do not of course mean that he did anything wrong in the technological sense: presumably he knew how to manoeuvre his ship in the right way.) He has kept his boat cunningly concealed, when it would have been better for humanity if it had been a sitting duck, he has kept the morale of his crew high when it would have been better if they had been cowardly and inefficient, and has aimed his torpedoes with deadly effect so as to do the maximum harm. Nevertheless, once the enemy commander is captured, or even perhaps before he is captured, our act-utilitarian sailor does the right thing in praising the enemy commander, behaving chivalrously towards him, giving him honour and so on, for he is powerfully influencing his own men to aspire to similar professional courage and efficiency, to the ultimate benefit of mankind.

What I have said in the last paragraph about the occasional utility of praising harmful actions applies, I think, even when the utilitarian is speaking to other utilitarians. It applies even more when, as is more usually the case, the utilitarian is speaking to a predominantly non-utilitarian audience. To take an extreme case, suppose that the utilitarian is speaking to people who live in a society governed by a form of magical taboo ethics. He may consider that though on occasion keeping to the taboos does harm, on the whole the tendency of the taboo ethics is more beneficial than the sort of moral anarchy into which these people might fall if their reverence for their taboos was weakened. While, therefore, he would recognize that the system of taboos which governed these people's conduct was markedly inferior to a utilitarian ethic, nevertheless he might also recognize that these people's cultural background was such that they could not easily be persuaded to adopt a utilitarian ethic. He will, therefore, on act-utilitarian grounds, distribute his praise and blame in such a way as to strengthen, not to weaken, the system of taboo.

In an ordinary society we do not find such an extreme situation. Many people can be got to adopt a utilitarian, or almost utilitarian, way of thought, but many cannot. We may consider whether it may not be better to throw our weight on the side of the prevailing traditional morality, rather than on the side of trying to improve it with the risk of weakening respect for morality altogether. Sometimes the answer to this question will be 'yes', and sometimes 'no'. As Sidgwick said:[1]

The doctrine that Universal Happiness is the ultimate *standard* must not be understood to imply that Universal Benevolence is . . . always the best *motive* of action. For . . . it is not necessary that the end which gives the criterion of rightness should always be the end at which we consciously aim: and if experience shows that the general happiness will be more satisfactorily attained if men frequently act from other motives than pure universal philanthropy, it is obvious that these other motives are to be preferred on Utilitarian principles.

In general, we may note, it is always dangerous to influence a person contrary to his conviction of what is right. More harm may be done in weakening his regard for duty than would be saved by preventing the particular action in question. Furthermore, to quote Sidgwick again, "any particular existing moral rule, though not the ideally best even for such beings, as existing men under the existing circumstances,

[1] *Methods of Ethics*, p. 413.

may yet be the best that they can be got to obey".[1] We must also remember that some motives are likely to be present in excess rather than defect: in which case, however necessary they may be, it is not expedient to praise them. It is obviously useful to praise altruism, even though this is not pure generalized benevolence, the treating of oneself as neither more nor less important than anyone else, simply because most people err on the opposite side, from too much self-love and not enough altruism. It is, similarly, inexpedient to praise self-love, important though this is when it is kept in due proportion. In short, to quote Sidgwick once more, "in distributing our praise of human qualities, on utilitarian principles, we have to consider not primarily the usefulness of the quality, but the usefulness of the praise".[2]

Most men, we must never forget, are not act-utilitarians, and do not use the words 'good' and 'bad', when applied to agents or to motives, quite in the way which has here been recommended. When a man says that another is wicked he may even be saying something of a partly metaphysical or superstitious connotation. He may be saying that there is something like a yellow stain on the other man's soul. Of course he would not think this quite literally. If you asked him whether souls could be coloured, or whether yellow was a particularly abhorrent colour, he would of course laugh at you. His views about sin and wickedness may be left in comfortable obscurity. Nevertheless the things he *does* say may indeed entail something *like* the yellow stain view. 'Wicked' has thus come to have much more force than the utilitarian 'likely to be very harmful' or 'probably a menace'. To stigmatize a man as wicked is not, as things are, just to make men wary of him, but to make him the object of a peculiar and very powerful abhorrence, over and above the

[1] *Ibid.* p. 469.
[2] *Ibid.* p. 428.

natural abhorrence one has from a dangerous natural object such as a typhoon or an octopus. And it may well be to the act-utilitarian's advantage, *qua* act-utilitarian, to acquiesce in this way of talking when he is in the company of non-utilitarians. He himself will not believe in yellow stains in souls, or anything like it. *Tout comprendre c'est tout pardonner*; a man is the result of heredity and environment. Nevertheless the utilitarian may influence behaviour in the way he desires by using 'wicked' in a quasi-superstitious way. Similarly a man about to be boiled alive by cannibals may usefully say that an imminent eclipse is a sign of the gods' displeasure at the proposed culinary activities. We have seen that in a completely utilitarian society the utility of praise of an agent's motives does not always go along with the utility of the action. Still more may this be so in a non-utilitarian society.

I cannot stress too often the importance of Sidgwick's distinction between the utility of an action and the utility of praise or blame of it, for many fallacious 'refutations' of utilitarianism depend for their plausibility on confusing the two things.

Thus A. N. Prior[1] quotes the nursery rhyme:

> For want of a nail
>   The shoe was lost;
> For want of a shoe
>   The horse was lost;
> For want of a horse
>   The rider was lost;
> For want of a rider
>   The battle was lost;
> For want of a battle
>   The kingdom was lost;
> And all for the want
>   Of a horse-shoe nail.

[1] 'The consequences of actions', *Aristotelian Society Supplementary Volume* 30 (1956) 91–9. See p. 95.

So it was all the blacksmith's fault! But, says Prior, it is surely hard to place on the smith's shoulders the responsibility for the loss of the kingdom. This is no objection, however, to act-utilitarianism. The utilitarian could quite consistently say that it would be useless to blame the blacksmith, or at any rate to blame him more than for any other more or less trivial case of 'bad maintenance'. The blacksmith had no reason to believe that the fate of the kingdom would depend on one nail. If you blame him you may make him neurotic and in future even more horses may be badly shod.

Moreover, says Prior, the loss of the kingdom was just as much the fault of someone whose negligence led to there being one fewer cannon in the field. If it had not been for this other piece of negligence the blacksmith's negligence would not have mattered. Whose was *the* responsibility? The act-utilitarian will quite consistently reply that the notion of *the* responsibility is a piece of metaphysical nonsense and should be replaced by 'Whom would it be useful to blame?' And in the case of such a close battle, no doubt it would be useful to blame quite a lot of people though no one very much. Unlike, for example, the case where a battle was lost on account of the general getting drunk, where considerable blame of one particular person would clearly be useful.

"But wouldn't a man go mad if he really tried to take the whole responsibility of everything upon himself in this way?" asks Prior. Clearly he would. The blacksmith must not mortify himself with morbid thoughts about his carelessness. He must remember that his carelessness was of the sort that is usually trivial, and that a lot of other people were equally careless. The battle was just a very close thing. But this refusal to blame himself, or blame himself very much, is surely consistent with the recognition that his action was *in fact* very wrong, that much harm would have been prevented if he had acted otherwise. Though if other people, e.g. the man whose fault it was that the extra cannon did not turn up, had acted differently, then the blacksmith's action would have in fact not been very wrong, though it would have been no more and no less blameworthy. A very wrong action is usually very blameworthy, but on some occasions, like the present one, a very wrong action can be hardly blameworthy at all. This seems paradoxical at first, but paradox disappears when we remember Sidgwick's distinction between the utility of an action and utility of praise of it.

The idea that a consistent utilitarian would go mad with worry about the various effects of his actions is perhaps closely connected with a curious argument against utilitarianism to be found in Baier's book *The Moral Point of View*.[1] Baier holds that (act-) utilitarianism must be rejected because it entails that we should never relax, that we should use up every available minute in good works, and we do not ordinarily think that this is so. The utilitarian has two effective replies. The first is that perhaps what we ordinarily think is false. Perhaps a rational investigation would lead us to the conclusion that we should relax much less than we do. The second reply is that act-utilitarianism premisses do not entail that we should never relax. Maybe relaxing and doing few good works today increases threefold our capacity to do good works tomorrow. So relaxation and play can be defended even if we ignore, as we should not, their intrinsic pleasures.

I beg the reader, therefore, if ever he is impressed by any alleged refutation of act-utilitarianism, to bear in mind the distinction between the rightness or wrongness of an action and the goodness or badness of the agent, and Sidgwick's correlative and most important distinction between the

[1] K. E. M. Baier, *The Moral Point of View* (Cornell University Press, Ithaca, New York, 1958), pp. 203–4.

utility of an action and the utility of praise or blame of it. The neglect of this distinction is one of the commonest causes of fallacious refutations of act-utilitarianism.

It is also necessary to remember that we are here considering utilitarianism as a *normative* system. The fact that it has consequences which conflict with some of our particular moral judgements need not be decisive against it. In science general principles must be tested by reference to particular facts of observation. In ethics we may well take the opposite attitude, and test our particular moral attitudes by reference to more general ones. The utilitarian can contend that since his principles rests on something so simple and natural as generalized benevolence it is more securely founded than our particular feelings, which may be subtly distorted by analogies with similar looking (but in reality totally different) types of case, and by all sorts of hangovers from traditional and uncritical ethical thinking.

If, of course, act-utilitarianism were put forward as a descriptive systematization of how ordinary men, or even we ourselves in our unreflective and uncritical moments, actually think about ethics, then of course it is easy to refute and I have no wish to defend it. Similarly again if it is put forward not as a *descriptive* theory but as an *explanatory* one.

John Plamenatz, in his *English Utilitarians*, seems to hold that utilitarianism "is destroyed and no part of it left standing".[1] This is apparently on the ground that the utilitarian *explanation* of social institutions will not work: that we cannot *explain* various institutions as having come about because they lead to the maximum happiness. In this monograph I am not concerned with what our moral customs and institutions in fact are, and still less am I concerned with the question of *why* they are as they in fact are. I am concerned with a certain view about what they *ought* to be. The correct-

[1] *The English Utilitarians*, 2nd edn (Blackwell, Oxford, 1966), p. 145.

ness of an ethical doctrine, when it is interpreted as recommendatory, is quite independent of its truth when it is interpreted as descriptive and of its truth when it is interpreted as explanatory. In fact it is precisely because a doctrine is false as description and as explanation that it becomes important as a possible recommendation.

8. Simple application of game-theory technique

So far I hope that I have shown that act-utilitarianism, as a normative theory of ethics, is not so simple-minded a doctrine as its critics seem to suppose, and that it escapes some of the usual refutations. I wish now to analyse a type of situation which has in the past proved difficult for the act-utilitarian to handle, but for which some very simple techniques of the theory of games seem to provide the solution.

R. B. Brandt[1] considers the case of a utilitarian in wartime England, and it is supposed that there is a governmental request that a maximum temperature of 50° F. should be maintained in homes, so as to conserve gas and electricity. A utilitarian Frenchman who is resident in England might conceivably reason as follows: "It is very unlikely that the vast majority of Englishmen will not comply with this request. But it will do no harm at all if a few people, such as myself, live in a temperature of 70° F. And it will do these few people a lot of good for their comfort. Therefore the general happiness will be increased by my using enough electricity and gas to make myself comfortable." The Frenchman thus decides to use the electricity and gas. Of course in practice such a decision might not make the Frenchman happier. If he was a decent person, normally brought up, he would feel very considerable twinges of

[1] *Ethical Theory*, p. 389.

conscience. But suppose the Frenchman is an absolutely single-minded out and out utilitarian. What then?

The act-utilitarian will have to agree that *if the Frenchman's behaviour could be kept secret* then he ought in this case to use the electricity and gas. But the Frenchman should also agree that he should be condemned and punished if he were found out. There would indeed, as Brandt points out, be a horrible outcry if it became known that members of the Cabinet, who were aware of the willingness of most people to sacrifice and thus knew that electricity and gas were in reasonably good supply, ignored their own regulation. In this case, too, the utilitarian calculation would indeed be different if we assumed that the behaviour of the members of the Cabinet would leak out. Moreover the utilitarian would hold that in this case there would be good utilitarian reasons (especially in a generally non-utilitarian society) for *condemning* the Cabinet. We must recollect the distinction between utility of an action and utility of praise or blame of it. However, independently of this last point, we may agree that Brandt has produced a case in which the utilitarian is likely to conflict with common sense ethics. The utilitarian, to be consistent, must be willing to say, "So much the worse for common sense ethics!"

Brandt further objects that if *everyone* followed the Frenchman's reasoning disastrous results would follow. This objection fails to recognize that the Frenchman would have used as an empirical premiss in his calculation the proposition that very few people would be likely to reason as he does. They would very likely be adherents of a traditional, non-utilitarian morality.

How would the Frenchman reason if he were living in a society composed entirely of convinced and rational act-utilitarians like himself? He is in the situation of not knowing how to plan his actions unless he has premisses about what other people will do, and each of them will not know how to plan his actions unless he knows what the rest of the people (including the Frenchman) will do. There is a circularity in the situation which cries out for the technique of game theory.

There are three types of possibility: (a) he can decide to obey the government's request; (b) he can decide not to obey the government's request; (c) he can decide to give himself a certain probability of not obeying the government's request, e.g. by deciding to throw dice and disobey the government's request if and only if he got a certain number of successive sixes.

To decide to do something of type (c) is to adopt what in game theory is called 'a mixed strategy'. On plausible assumptions it would turn out that the best result would be attained if each member of the act-utilitarian society were to give himself a very small probability p of disobeying the government's request. In practice p is very difficult to calculate, and since it is likely to be very small, in practice the act-utilitarian will adopt alternative (a). Indeed if the trouble of calculating p outweighed the probable benefit of adopting the mixed strategy, and we took this into account, we should have to plump for alternative (a) anyway.

Let us see how this probability p could be calculated. Even if the matter is of little practical importance it is of interest for the theoretical understanding of ethics.

Let m be the number of people in the community. Let $f(n)$ be the national damage done by exactly n people disobeying the government's request; it will be an increasing function of n. Now if each member of the community gives himself a probability p of disobeying the edict it is easy to determine, as functions of p, the probabilities p_1, $p_2,...p_m$ of exactly 1, 2,...m persons respectively disobeying the edict. Let a be the personal benefit to each person of disobeying the edict. I am, of course, supposing what is perhaps a fiction, that numerical values can be given to $f(n)$ and to a. Then if V is the total probable benefit to the community we have

$$V = p_1(a-f(1))+p_2(2a-f(2))+p_3(3a-f(3))+\ldots$$
$$p_m(ma-f(m)).$$

If we know the function $f(n)$ we can calculate the value of p for which $\dfrac{\mathrm{d}V}{\mathrm{d}p} = 0$. This will give the value of p which maximizes V.

As I said, the matter is of theoretical rather than practical importance, as in the sort of case which I have in mind p will be so near to zero that the act-utilitarian would not bother to calculate but would just obey the government's request. No doubt special examples of moral decision could be devised in which a not too small value of p would be obtained. This type of reasoning seems to be important more for the theoretical insight it affords than for its potentiality for practical guidance.[1]

It might be thought that this symmetrical solution by means of mixed strategies implies some sort of rule-utilitarianism.[2] For will a group of act-utilitarians have any empirical basis for assuming that they will all adopt a symmetrical solution to the problem? Of course if David Lyons is right that rule-utilitarianism and act-utilitarianism collapse into one another, the problem disappears. However, as I remarked on p. 11 above, I cannot see how to apply Lyons' argument

[1] The adoption of a mixed strategy would seem to provide the solution (in theory) to the garden watering example in A. K. Stout's article, 'But suppose everyone did the same', *Australasian Journal of Philosophy* 32 (1954) 1–29.

[2] See perceptive remarks by M. A. Kaplan, in his note 'Restricted utilitarianism', *Ethics* 71 (1960–1) 301–2 and David Braybrooke, 'The choice between utilitarianisms', *American Philosophical Quarterly* 4 (1967) 28–38.

to the sort of situation in which what one person ought to do depends on what others ought to do and vice versa. This sort of situation requires special treatment.

The clue lies in the notion of a *convention*, which has been elucidated in an important book by David K. Lewis.[1] Lewis, in turn, makes use of Thomas C. Schelling's study of 'co-ordination games',[2] which suggests that two agents can co-ordinate their activities without rules. For example, two parachutists, who have been dropped in enemy country and need to rendezvous, will both make their way to a bridge when this is the only salient feature on the map. The act-utilitarian will have to take this propensity to co-ordinate behaviour as an empirical fact about human beings which each will legitimately take into account when planning his strategy. Lewis shows that the notion of a convention is prior to that of a rule, and so I think that a reliance by the act-utilitarian on conventions need not turn him into a rule-utilitarian or even into a Kantian. Lewis has made a remarkable analysis of one type of alleged objection to act-utilitarianism, making use of his theory of convention, in an article 'Utilitarianism and truthfulness'.[3]

Even if the solution to the present difficulty *were* rule-utilitarianism it would be a rule-utilitarianism (or perhaps Kantianism) which would be markedly different from those which have generally been put forward, since it would be applicable *only* in those situations in which all the agents are utilitarians. My sort of utilitarian will normally think that he ought to act when he is in a predominantly non-utilitarian society in a way which is different from the way in which

[1] David K. Lewis, *Convention* (Harvard University Press, Cambridge, Mass., 1969).

[2] Thomas C. Schelling, *The Strategy of Conflict* (Harvard University Press, Cambridge, Mass., 1960).

[3] *Australasian Journal of Philosophy* 50 (1972) 17–19. This is in reply to an argument by D. H. Hodgson, *Consequences of Utilitarianism* (Oxford University Press, London, 1967), pp. 38–46.

he ought to act when he is in a utilitarian society. Furthermore, even in the case of a society of like-minded utilitarians, the mixed strategy solution makes it importantly different from the usual 'all or none' varieties of rule-utilitarianism.

9. Utilitarianism and the future

The chief persuasive argument in favour of utilitarianism has been that the dictates of any deontological ethics will always, on some occasions, lead to the existence of misery that could, on utilitarian principles, have been prevented. Thus if the deontologist says that promises always should be kept (or even if, like Ross, he says that there is a *prima facie* duty to keep them) we may confront him with a situation like the following, the well-known 'desert island promise': I have promised a dying man on a desert island, from which subsequently I alone am rescued, to give his hoard of gold to the South Australian Jockey Club. On my return I give it to the Royal Adelaide Hospital, which, we may suppose, badly needs it for a new X-ray machine. Could anybody deny that I had done rightly without being open to the charge of heartlessness? (Remember that the promise was known only to me, and so my action will not in this case weaken the general confidence in the social institution of promising.) Think of the persons dying of painful tumours who could have been saved by the desert island gold!

"But", the deontologist may still object, "it is my doctrine which is the humane one. You have accused me of inhumanity because I sometimes cause avoidable misery for the sake of keeping a rule. But it is these very rules, which you regard as so cold and inhuman, which safeguard mankind from the most awful atrocities. In the interests of future generations are we to allow millions to die of starvation, or still more millions to be sent to forced labour? Is it not this very consequentialist mentality which is at the root of the vast injustices which we see in the world today?" Two replies are relevant. In the first place the man who says this sort of thing may or may not be interested in the welfare of future generations. It is perfectly possible not to have the sentiment of generalized benevolence but to be moved by a localized benevolence. When this is localized in space we get the ethics of the tribe or the race: when it is localized in time we get an ethics of the present day and generation. It may well be that atrocities carried out for the sake of a Utopian future repel some people *simply* because they mortgage the present for the sake of the future. Here we have a difference about ultimate ends, and in this case I cannot accuse my opponent of being either confused or superstitious, though I may accuse him of being limited in his vision. Why should not future generations matter as much as present ones? To deny it is to be temporally parochial. If it is objected that future generations will only *probably* exist, I reply: would not the objector take into account a probably existing *present* population on a strange island before using it for bomb tests?

In the second place, however, the opponent of utilitarianism may have a perfectly disinterested benevolence, save for his regard for the observance of rules as such. Future generations may in fact mean as much to him as present ones. To him the utilitarian may reply as follows. If it were known to be true, as a question of fact, that measures which caused misery and death to tens of millions today *would* result in saving from greater misery and from death hundreds of millions in the future, and if this were the only way in which it could be done, then it *would* be right to cause these necessary atrocities. The case is surely no different in principle from that of the battalion commander who sacrifices a patrol to save a company. Where the tyrants who cause atrocities for the sake of Utopia are wrong is, surely, on the plain question of fact, and on confusing probabilities with certainties. After all, one would have to be *very sure* that future generations would be saved still greater misery before one embarked on such a tyrannical programme. One thing we should now know about the future is that large-scale predictions are impossible. Could Jeremy Bentham or Karl Marx (to take two very different political theorists) have foreseen the atom bomb? Could they have foreseen automation? Can we foresee the technology of the next century? Where the future is so dim a man must be mad who would sacrifice the present in a big way for the sake of it. Moreover even if the future were clear to us, it is very improbable that large scale atrocities could be beneficial. We must not forget the immense side effects: the brutalization of the people who ordered the atrocities and carried them out. We can, in fact, agree with the most violent denouncer of atrocities carried out in the name of Utopia without sacrificing our act-utilitarian principles. Indeed there are the best of act-utilitarian reasons for denouncing atrocities. But it is empirical facts, and empirical facts only, which will lead the utilitarian to say this.

The future, I have remarked, is dim, largely because the potentialities of technological advance are unknown to us. This consideration both increases the attractiveness of a utilitarian ethics (because of the built-in flexibility of such an ethics) and increases the difficulty of applying such an ethics.

Normally the utilitarian is able to assume that the remote effects of his actions tend tapidly to zero, like the ripples on a pond after a stone has been thrown into it. This assumption normally seems quite a plausible one. Suppose that a man is deciding whether to seduce his neighbour's wife. On utilitarian grounds it seems pretty obvious that such an act would be wrong, for the unhappiness which it is likely to cause in the short term will probably be only too obvious. The man need not consider the possibility that one of his remote descendants, if he seduces the woman, will be a great benefactor of the human race. Such a possibility is not all that improbable, considering the very likely vast number of descendants after a good many generations, but it is no more probable than the possibility that one of his remote descendants will do great harm to the human race, or that one of the descendants from a more legitimate union would benefit the human race. It seems plausible that the long-term probable benefits and costs of his alternative actions are likely to be negligible or to cancel one another out.

An obviously important case in which, if he were a utilitarian, a person would have to consider effects into the far future, perhaps millions of years, would be that of a statesman who was contemplating engaging in nuclear warfare, if there were some probability, even a small one, that this war might end in the destruction of the entire human race. (Even a war less drastic than this might have important consequences into the fairly far future, say hundreds of years.) Similar long term catastrophic consequences must be envisaged in planning flight to other planets, if there is any probability, even quite a small one, that these planets possess viruses or bacteria, to which terrestrial organisms would have no immunity.

The progress of science and technology could yield many more cases which might pose dramatic problems to the moralist. Consider the moral problems which would be set by a spectacular innovation in the field of positive eugenics,[1]

---

[1] Positive eugenics is a matter of encouraging breeding by those with desirable genes, whereas negative eugenics is a matter of discouraging breeding of those with undesirable genes. In the present state of knowledge of human genetics, at least, the latter is much more scientifically respectable than the former. For a spectacular suggestion in the field of positive eugenics, see the book *Out of the Night* (Gollancz, London, 1936) by the American geneticist H. J. Muller. For a popular account of the biological difficulties which beset the idea of positive eugenics, see P. B. Medawar, *The Future of Man* (Methuen, London, 1959), lectures 3 and 4.

or perhaps of direct tampering with the human genetic material, or of a spectacular discovery which would enable the life span of man to be prolonged indefinitely. (For example, would the realization of the last possibility imply the rightness of universal euthanasia?) Again, suppose that it became possible to design an ultra-intelligent machine[1] (superior in intelligence to any human) which could then design a yet more intelligent machine which could ... (and so on).

Consider positive eugenics first. Suppose that it did one day turn out that by methods of positive eugenics, it became possible markedly to increase the intelligence of the whole human race, without using tyrannical or unpleasant means and without reducing the genetic diversity of the species. (There are important biological advantages in diversity.) Ought a utilitarian to approve of such a measure? Clearly something will depend on whether he is a hedonistic or an ideal utilitarian. The ideal utilitarian may have an intrinsic preference for more intelligent states of mind. However the hedonistic utilitarian might agree with the ideal one if he thought that intelligence was extrinsically valuable, for example if he thought that wars and poverty were due mainly to stupidity, and perhaps if he thought that more avenues for obtaining pleasure were open to intelligent people.

Even more interesting ethical issues arise if we imagine that biological engineering went so far as to enable the production of a higher species of man altogether. Similar issues arise also if we imagine that it becomes possible to produce an ultra-intelligent artefact which possesses consciousness. (This is not the place to enter into the deep metaphysical issues which arise out of the question of whether a

[1] See, for example, I. J. Good, 'Speculations concerning the first ultra-intelligent machine', *Advances in Computers*, vol. 6, Academic Press, New York, 1965.

conscious artefact is possible or not.) Let an entity which is either a member of the envisaged superior species or is an ultra-intelligent conscious artefact be conveniently referred to as 'a superman'. What might a utilitarian's attitude be towards possible actions which would lead to the production of a superman? It is quite possible that there should be a kind of utilitarian who valued only the happiness of his own species and was perfectly indifferent to that of higher and lower species. He might even envisage the superman with fear and hatred. Such a man's ethics would be analogous to the ethics of the tribe. Suppose alternatively that he were an ideal or quasi-ideal utilitarian, who thought that it was better to be Socrates dissatisfied than a fool satisfied. Should he similarly yield ethical precedence to the superman?

At present there is much less possibility of practical disagreement between those who concern themselves with the happiness of all sentient beings. As regards inferior beings, there is indeed a possibility of serious disagreement over the morality of such things as 'factory farming'. But if it became possible to control our evolution in such a way as to develop a superior species, then the difference between a species morality and a morality of all sentient beings would become very much more of a live issue.

10. Utilitarianism and justice

So far, I have done my best to state utilitarianism in a way which is conceptually clear and to rebut many common objections to it. At the time I wrote the earlier edition of this monograph I did so as a pretty single-minded utilitarian myself. It seemed to me then that since the utilitarian principle expressed the attitude of generalized benevolence, anyone who rejected utilitarianism would have to be hard hearted, i.e. to some extent non-benevolent, or else would have to be the prey of conceptual confusion or an unthinking adherent of traditional ways of thought, or perhaps be an adherent of some religious system of ethics, which could be undermined by metaphysical criticism. Admittedly utilitarianism does have consequences which are incompatible with the common moral consciousness, but I tended to take the view "so much the worse for the common moral consciousness". That is, I was inclined to reject the common methodology of testing general ethical principles by seeing how they square with our feelings in particular instances.

After all, one may feel somewhat as follows. What is the purpose of morality? (Answering this question is to make a moral judgement. To think that one could answer the question "What is the purpose of morality?" without making a moral judgement would be to condone the naturalistic fallacy, the fallacy of deducing an 'ought' from an 'is'.) Suppose that we say, as it is surely at least tempting to do, that the purpose of morality is to subserve the general happiness. Then it immediately seems to follow that we ought to reject any putative moral rule, or any particular moral feeling, which conflicts with the utilitarian principle. It is undeniable that we do have anti-utilitarian moral feelings in particular cases, but perhaps they should be discounted as far as possible, as due to our moral conditioning in childhood. (The weakness of this line of thought is that approval of the general principle of utilitarianism may be due to moral conditioning too. And even if benevolence were in some way a 'natural', not an 'artificial', attitude, this consideration could at best have persuasive force, without any clear rationale. To argue from the naturalness to the correctness of a moral attitude would be to commit the naturalistic fallacy.) Nevertheless in some moods the general principle of utilitarianism may recommend itself to us so much the more than do particular moral precepts, precisely because it *is* so general. We may therefore feel inclined to reject an ethical methodology which implies that we should test our general principles by our reactions in particular cases. Rather, we may come to feel, we should test our reactions in particular cases by reference to the most general principles. The analogy with science is not a good one, since it is not far off the truth to say that observation statements are more firmly based than the theories they test.[1] But why should our more particular moral feelings be more worthy of notice than our more generalized ones? That there should be a disanalogy between ethics and science is quite plausible if we accept a non-cognitivist theory of meta-ethics.

The utilitarian, then, will test his particular feelings by reference to his general principle, and not the general principle by reference to his particular feelings. Now while I have some tendency to take this point of view (and if I had not I would not have been impelled to state and defend utilitarianism as a system of normative ethics) I have also some tendency to feel the opposite, that we should sometimes test our general principles by how we feel about particular applications of them. (I am a bit like G. E. Moore in his reply to C. L. Stevenson,[2] where he feels both that he is right and Stevenson wrong and that he is wrong and Stevenson is right. My own indecisiveness may be harder to resolve, since in my case it is a matter of feeling, rather than intellect, which is involved.)

It is not difficult to show that utilitarianism could, in certain exceptional circumstances, have some very horrible consequences. In a very lucid and concise discussion note,[3] H. J. McCloskey has considered such a case. Suppose that the sheriff of a small town can prevent serious riots (in

[1] I say, 'not far off the truth' because observation statements are to some extent theory laden, and if they are laden with a bad theory we may have to reject them.
[2] See P. A. Schilpp (ed.), *The Philosophy of G. E. Moore* (Northwestern University Press, Evanston, Illinois, 1942), p. 554.
[3] H. J. McCloskey, 'A note on utilitarian punishment', *Mind* 72 (1963) 599.

which hundreds of people will be killed) only by 'framing' and executing (as a scapegoat) an innocent man. In actual cases of this sort the utilitarian will usually be able to agree with our normal moral feelings about such matters. He will be able to point out that there would be some possibility of the sheriff's dishonesty being found out, with consequent weakening of confidence and respect for law and order in the community, the consequences of which would be far worse even than the painful deaths of hundreds of citizens. But as McCloskey is ready to point out, the case can be presented in such a way that these objections do not apply. For example, it can be imagined that the sheriff could have first-rate empirical evidence that he will not be found out. So the objection that the sheriff *knows* that the man he 'frames' will be killed, whereas he has only probable belief that the riot will occur unless he frames the man, is not a sound one. Someone like McCloskey can always strengthen his story to the point that we would just have to admit that if utilitarianism is correct, then the sheriff must frame the innocent man. (McCloskey also has cogently argued that similar objectionable consequences are also implied by rule-utilitarianism. That is, an unjust *system* of punishment might be more *useful* than a just one. Hence even if rule-utilitarianism can clearly be distinguished from act-utilitarianism, a utilitarian will not be able to avoid offensive consequences of his theory by retreating from the 'act' form to the 'rule' form.) Now though a utilitarian might argue that it is empirically unlikely that some such situation as McCloskey envisages would ever occur, McCloskey will point out that it is *logically* possible that such a situation will arise. If the utilitarian rejects the unjust act (or system) he is clearly giving up his utilitarianism. McCloskey then remarks: "But as far as I know, only J. J. C. Smart among the contemporary utilitarians, is happy to adopt this 'solution'." Here I must lodge a mild protest. McCloskey's use of the word 'happy' surely makes me look a most reprehensible person. Even in my most utilitarian moods I am not *happy* about this consequence of utilitarianism. Nevertheless, however unhappy about it he may be, the utilitarian must admit that he draws the consequence that he might find himself in circumstances where he ought to be unjust. Let us hope that this is a logical possibility and not a factual one. In hoping thus I am not being inconsistent with utilitarianism, since any injustice causes misery and so can be justified only as the lesser of two evils. The fewer the situations in which the utilitarian is forced to choose the lesser of two evils, the better he will be pleased. One must not think of the utilitarian as the sort of person who you would not trust further than you could kick him. As a matter of untutored sociological observation, I should say that in general utilitarians are more than usually trustworthy people, and that the sort of people who might do you down are rarely utilitarians.

It is also true that we should probably dislike and fear a man who could bring himself to do the right utilitarian act in a case of the sort envisaged by McCloskey. Though the man in this case might have done the right utilitarian act, his act would betoken a toughness and lack of squeamishness which would make him a dangerous person. We must remember that people have egoistic tendencies as well as beneficent ones, and should such a person be tempted to act wrongly he could act very wrongly indeed. A utilitarian who remembers the possible moral weakness of men might quite consistently prefer to be the sort of person who would not always be able to bring himself to do the right utilitarian act and to surround himself by people who would be too squeamish to act in a utilitarian manner in such extreme cases.

No, I am not happy to draw the conclusion that McCloskey quite rightly says that the utilitarian must draw. But neither am I happy with the anti-utilitarian conclusion. For if a case really *did* arise in which injustice was the lesser of two evils (in terms of human happiness and misery), then the anti-utilitarian conclusion is a very unpalatable one too, namely that in some circumstances one must choose the greater misery, perhaps the *very much* greater misery, such as that of hundreds of people suffering painful deaths.

Still, to be consistent, the utilitarian must accept McCloskey's challenge. Let us hope that the sort of possibility which he envisages will always be no more than a logical possibility and will never become an actuality. At any rate, even though I have suggested that in ethics we should test particular feelings by general attitudes, McCloskey's example makes me somewhat sympathetic to the opposite point of view. Perhaps indeed it is too much to hope that there is *any* possible ethical system which will appeal to all sides of our nature and to all our moods.[1] It is perfectly possible to have conflicting attitudes within oneself. It is quite conceivable that there is *no* possible ethical theory which will be conformable with all our attitudes. If the theory is utilitarian, then the possibility that sometimes it would be right to commit injustice will be felt to be acutely unsatisfactory by someone with a normal civilized upbringing. If on the other hand it is not utilitarian but has deontological elements, then it will have the unsatisfactory implication that sometimes avoidable misery (perhaps very great avoidable misery) ought not to be avoided. It might be thought that some compromise theory, on the lines of Sir David Ross's, in which there is some 'balancing up' between considerations of utility and those of deontology, might provide an acceptable compro-

---

[1] J. W. N. Watkins considers this matter in his 'Negative utilitarianism', *Aristotelian Society Supp. Vol.* 67 (1963) 95–114. It is now apparent to me that my paper 'The methods of ethics and the methods of science', *Journal of Philosophy* 62 (1965) 344–9, on which the present section of this monograph is based, gives a misleading impression of Watkins's position in this respect.

mise. The trouble with this, however, is that such a 'balancing' may not be possible: one can easily feel pulled sometimes one way and sometimes the other. How can one 'balance' a serious injustice, on the one hand, and hundreds of painful deaths, on the other hand? Even if we disregard our purely self-interested attitudes, for the sake of interpersonal discussions, so as to treat ourselves neither more nor less favourably than other people, it is still possible that there is no ethical system which would be satisfactory to all men, or even to one man at different times. It is possible that something similar is the case with science, that no scientific theory (known or unknown) is correct. If so, the world is more chaotic than we believe and hope that it is. But even though the world is not chaotic, men's moral feelings may be. On anthropological grounds it is only too likely that these feelings are to some extent chaotic. Both as children and as adults, we have probably had many different moral conditionings, which can easily be incompatible with one another.

Meanwhile, among possible options, utilitarianism does have its appeal. With its empirical attitude to questions of means and ends it is congenial to the scientific temper and it has flexibility to deal with a changing world. This last consideration is, however, more self-recommendation than justification. For if flexibility is a recommendation, this is because of the utility of flexibility.

ACKNOWLEDGEMENTS

The foregoing is a revised version of my monograph *An Outline of a System of Utilitarian Ethics*, which was published in 1961 by the Melbourne University Press, with generous financial aid from the University of Adelaide. I should like to reiterate the expression of gratitude, which I made in the preface to the original edition, to the University of Adelaide, and to the officers of the Melbourne University Press, as well as to Professors A. G. N. Flew, R. M. Hare, J. C. Harsanyi, B. H. Medlin, D. H. Monro, and A. K. Stout, who had commented on earlier drafts of the monograph.

I am grateful to Mrs Patricia Skinner of the Cambridge University Press, for her suggestion that the revised edition be published together with a monograph by Bernard Williams.

In the years since I wrote the original pamphlet I have not been working a great deal in the field of ethics. I have therefore not made very extensive changes in the original. However I have made some attempt to deal with certain criticisms which in the intervening years have been made of utilitarianism in general, and sometimes of my ideas in particular, and I have made various deletions and additions. However, this falls far short of a complete re-thinking of the issues. The final section of this edition is based on parts of my paper 'The methods of science and the methods of ethics', *Journal of Philosophy* 62 (1965) 344–9.

I should like to acknowledge that over the years since the publication of the first edition I have benefited by suggestions in correspondence or conversation with many friends, including (as well as some of those already mentioned) Professors R. B. Brandt, David K. Lewis, H. J. McCloskey, Richmond H. Thomason, J. W. N. Watkins, Henry West and Bernard Williams, though probably they will feel that I have not benefited enough.

I am also very grateful to Professor R. M. Hare for inviting me to join with him in giving a graduate class on utilitarianism at Oxford in the Michaelmas Term of 1970.

I have added a bibliography, which I hope will be valuable especially for students (including post-graduate students). The literature on utilitarianism has grown to be so vast that I am uneasily aware that I must have omitted some references which ought to be in it, but I have tried to make it at least reasonably detailed.

A critique of utilitarianism

BERNARD WILLIAMS

> If we possess our *why* of life we can put up with almost any *how*. –
> Man does not strive after happiness; only the Englishman does that.
> Nietzsche, *The Twilight of the Idols*

1. Introductory

This essay is not designed as a reply to Smart's. It has been written after it, in knowledge of it, and from an opposed point of view, but it does not try to answer his arguments point for point, nor to cover just the same ground. Direct criticism of Smart's text is largely confined to parts of section 6, where I have tried to show that a certain ambiguity in Smart's defence of act-utilitarianism, as against other sorts, arises from a deep difficulty in the whole subject. I have not attempted, either, to give an account of all the important issues in the area, still less a critical survey of the major items in the literature; I have pursued those questions which seemed to me the most interesting and have deliberately left out a number of things which are often discussed. Like Smart, I have very largely treated utilitarianism as a system of personal morality rather than as a system of social or political decision, but I have tried to say something, very much in outline, about political aspects in section 7. The appearance of that subject at the end is not supposed to represent a judgement on its relative importance, but is due to two things: that I felt I had more to say about matters, such as those discussed in section 5, which bear most on the personal case; and that I think it important to come to the political area by a certain route, which involves the question "In whose hands does utilitarian decision lie?", and that route goes, I find, through the problems I consider in section 6 as arising for personal morality.

It is a merit of Smart's essay that it gives an account of utilitarianism which for the most part does not labour under

D

too many qualifications, and is only mildly apologetic. He thus stands in contrast to many modern writers whose utilitarianism is accommodated to a range of moral beliefs which many earlier utilitarians would probably have wanted to discard on the strength of utilitarianism. I agree with what in general is his stand (subject to the ambiguity I have mentioned, and which I discuss in section 6), that utilitarianism, properly understood and consistently carried through, is a *distinctive* way of looking at human action and morality. These distinctive characteristics he mostly seems to find agreeable, while to me some of them seem horrible. What is important, however (at least so far as these essays are concerned) is not whether he, or I, or the reader regard this or that as horrible, but what the implications, carefully considered, are of these principles for one's views of human nature and action, other people and society. Where I have offered examples, as particularly in section 3, the aim is not just to offer or elicit moral intuitions against which utilitarianism can be tested. Although in the end everyone has to reflect, in relation to questions like these, what he would be prepared to live with, the aim of the examples and their discussion is not just to ask a question about that and wait for the answer: rather, the aim is to lead into reflections which might show up in greater depth what would be involved in living with these ideas. The first question for philosophy is not "do you agree with utilitarianism's answer?" but "do you really accept utilitarianism's way of looking at the question?"

If utilitarianism is a distinctive moral outlook, that does not mean that there is just one way in which it is distinctive. If Smart's system is found by various critics, crass, or unjust, or muddled, or unrealistic, it may well be to different aspects of it that they are reacting, and I hope that my discussion will to some extent help to separate different strains of criticism of utilitarianism, and different features of utilitarian systems to which they apply. There are three features in particular of Smart's system which may attract different kinds of criticism and which raise different kinds of issue. For these, reluctantly, I shall use some labels – reluctantly, because the use of technical labels in such matters can be a way of freezing the discussion, before one starts, into postures of antique controversy. But in this subject it is probably more misleading not to announce one's terminology, since many different technical terms, and different uses of the same terms to mark different distinctions, have been applied to it, and any term one uses will probably turn out to have been used by some other writer in a different sense. I shall be following some, at least, well-established practice in saying of Smart's system that it is *consequentialist*, and that its consequentialism is both *eudaimonistic* and *direct*.

Any kind of utilitarianism is by definition consequentialist, but 'consequentialism' is the broader term, and in my use (though not in everybody's use, and in particular, not in Smart's) utilitarianism is *one sort* of consequentialism – the sort (distinguished in the next paragraph) which is specially concerned with happiness. What is meant by 'consequentialism' turns out to be a harder question than at first appears, and I shall be concerned with it in section 2. It is also in my view an important question, since I think that some of the unacceptable features of utilitarianism, and some which I shall be particularly concerned with, are to be traced to its general character as a form of consequentialism. Very roughly speaking, consequentialism is the doctrine that the moral value of any action always lies in its consequences, and that it is by reference to their consequences that actions, and indeed such things as institutions, laws and practices, are to be justified if they can be justified at all.

To say, next, that the system is *eudaimonistic* is to say that what it regards as the desirable feature of actions is that they should increase or maximize people's *happiness*, as distinguished from certain other goods at which, according to some consequentialists, it is independently worth aiming our actions. I shall not introduce any separate term to mark the view that the preferred value is *pleasure*, or again, *satisfaction*. Instead of talking about amounts of happiness, I shall sometimes use the economists' phrase, and speak of an increase or decrease in (people's) *utility*; and I shall in general assume, along with most modern writers in philosophy and economics, that in talking of happiness or utility one is talking about people's desires or preferences and their getting what they want or prefer, rather than about some sensation of pleasure or happiness. I say a little more about these matters in sections 2 and 3. The few remarks I have to make on the notorious problems of comparing and adding utilities, I have left to section 7; and for a good deal of the earlier discussion I have gone on as though this were not a problem. This is false, but the full force of its falsehood is felt, necessarily, at the level of social decision. It would be idle to pretend that in many more restricted connexions we had *no idea* what course would lead to greater happiness, and in earlier parts of the essay I have confined myself to difficulties which arise even when we can take that question as settled.

I shall rarely have to use the cumbrous term 'eudaimonistic' again, since I shall use the word 'utilitarianism' indeed to mean 'eudaimonistic consequentialism'. This is not Smart's practice, who uses the word 'utilitarianism' in the broader sense (and the phrase 'ideal utilitarianism' to refer to forms of consequentialism not exclusively concerned with happiness). His defence, indeed, ranges over these other sorts of consequentialism, but for much of the time he is concerned with what, in my narrower definition, is utilitarianism, that is to say, with consequentialism aimed at happiness. His various appeals to the principle of *benevolence* seem in particular to relate to that.

The term *direct* I use – putting it, again, very roughly – to mean that the consequential value which is the concern of morality is attached directly to particular actions, rather than to rules or practices under which decisions are taken without further reference to consequences; the latter sort of view is *indirect* consequentialism. The distinction, or one very like it, is often labelled, as it is by Smart, as a distinction between *act*-utilitarianism and *rule*-utilitarianism. I am sorry to have used a different terminology from Smart within the same covers, but in each case it proves simpler for my own purposes to do so; in the present matter, the term 'rule-utilitarianism' is less than useful, particularly because I am concerned with the indirect value of various sorts of things besides rules, such as dispositions. Like most other distinctions in this field, that between direct and indirect utilitarianism is easier to see at first glance than later, and it raises many complications. I consider some in section 6. I think, as Smart to some extent does, that forms of utilitarianism which help themselves too liberally to the resources of indirectness lose their utilitarian rationale and end up as vanishingly forms of utilitarianism at all. Whether that is so is not just a question of nomenclature or classification – such a question, in itself, would be of no interest at all. It is a question of the *point* of utilitarianism.[1]

This essay is concerned with utilitarianism, and in so far as it goes into consequentialism in general, this is only in order to suggest that some undesirable features of utilitarianism follow from its general consequentialist structure. Others follow more specifically from the nature of its concern with happiness. I shall say something about that,

---

[1] I have offered some brief arguments specifically related to that in *Morality: An Introduction to Ethics* (Harper and Row, New York, 1972; Penguin Books, Harmondsworth, 1973). Although there is some overlap between that treatment and the present essay, I have in general tried to develop rather different points.

and about the relations between direct and indirect forms of utilitarianism. I shall consider the uneasy relations of utilitarianism to certain other values which people either more or less optimistic than Smart might consider to have something seriously to do with human life. One value which has caused particular discomfort to utilitarianism is *justice*. I shall say a little about that in section 7, but I shall be more concerned with something rather different, *integrity*. I shall try to show something to which Smart's system indeed bears silent witness, that utilitarianism cannot hope to make sense, at any serious level, of integrity. It cannot do that for the very basic reason that it can make only the most superficial sense of human desire and action at all; and hence only very poor sense of what was supposed to be its own speciality, happiness.

2. The structure of consequentialism

No one can hold that everything, of whatever category, that has value, has it in virtue of its consequences. If that were so, one would just go on for ever, and there would be an obviously hopeless regress. That regress would be hopeless even if one takes the view, which is not an absurd view, that although men set themselves ends and work towards them, it is very often not really the supposed end, but the effort towards it on which they set value – that they travel, not really in order to arrive (for as soon as they have arrived they set out for somewhere else), but rather they choose somewhere to arrive, in order to travel. Even on that view, not everything would have consequential value; what would have non-consequential value would in fact be travelling, even though people had to think of travelling as having the consequential value, and something else – the destination – the non-consequential value.

If not everything that has value has it in virtue of consequences, then presumably there are some types of thing which have non-consequential value, and also some particular things that have such value because they are instances of those types. Let us say, using a traditional term, that anything that has that sort of value, has *intrinsic* value.[1] I take it to be the central idea of consequentialism that the only kind of thing that has intrinsic value is states of affairs, and that anything else that has value has it because it conduces to some intrinsically valuable state of affairs.

How much, however, does this say? Does it succeed in distinguishing consequentialism from anything else? The trouble is that the term 'state of affairs' seems altogether too permissive to exclude anything: may not the obtaining of absolutely anything be represented formally as a state of affairs? A Kantian view of morality, for instance, is usually thought to be opposed to consequentialism, if any is; at the very least, if someone were going to show that Kantianism collapsed into consequentialism, it should be the product of a long and unobvious argument, and not just happen at the drop of a definition. But on the present account it looks as though Kantianism can be made instantly into a kind of consequentialism – a kind which identifies the states of affairs that have intrinsic value (or at least intrinsic moral value) as those that consist of actions being performed for duty's sake.[2] We need something more to our specification if it is to be the specification of anything distinctly consequentialist.

The point of saying that consequentialism ascribes intrinsic value to states of affairs is rather to *contrast* states of

---

[1] The terminology of things 'being valuable', 'having intrinsic value', etc., is not meant to beg any questions in general value-theory. Non-cognitive theories, such as Smart's, should be able to recognize the distinctions made here.

[2] A point noted by Smart, p. 13.

affairs with other candidates for having such value: in particular, perhaps, actions. A distinctive mark of consequentialism might rather be this, that it regards the value of actions as always consequential (or, as we may more generally say, derivative), and not intrinsic. The value of actions would then lie in their causal properties, of producing valuable states of affairs; or if they did not derive their value in this simple way, they would derive it in some more roundabout way, as for instance by being expressive of some motive, or in accordance with some rule, whose operation in society conduced to desirable states of affairs. (The lengths to which such indirect derivations can be taken without wrecking the point of consequentialism is something we shall be considering later.)

To insist that what has intrinsic value are states of affairs and not actions seems to come near an important feature of consequentialism. Yet it may be that we have still not hit exactly what we want, and that the restriction is now too severe. Surely *some* actions, compatibly with consequentialism, might have intrinsic value? This is a question which has a special interest for utilitarianism, that is to say, the form of consequentialism concerned particularly with happiness. Traditionally utilitarians have tended to regard happiness or, again, pleasure, as experiences or sensations which were related to actions and activity as effect to cause; and, granted that view, utilitarianism will indeed see the value of all action as derivative, intrinsic value being reserved for the experiences of happiness. But that view of the relations between action and either pleasure or happiness is widely recognized to be inadequate. To say that a man finds certain actions or activity pleasant, or that they make him happy, or that he finds his happiness in them, is certainly not always to say that they induce certain sensations in him, and in the case of happiness, it is doubtful whether that is ever what is meant. Rather it means such things (among others) as that he enjoys doing these things for their own sake. It would trivialize the discussion of utilitarianism to tie it by definition to inadequate conceptions of happiness or pleasure, and we must be able to recognize as versions of utilitarianism those which, as most modern versions do, take as central some notion such as *satisfaction*, and connect that criterially with such matters as the activities which a man will freely choose to engage in. But the activities which a man engages in for their own sake are activities in which he finds intrinsic value. So any specification of consequentialism which logically debars action or activity from having intrinsic value will be too restrictive even to admit the central case, utilitarianism, so soon as that takes on a more sophisticated and adequate conception of its basic value of happiness.

So far then, we seem to have one specification of consequentialism which is too generous to exclude anything, and another one which is too restrictive to admit even the central case. These difficulties arise from either admitting without question actions among desirable states of affairs, or blankly excluding all actions from the state of affairs category. This suggests that we shall do better by looking at the interrelations between states of affairs and actions.

It will be helpful, in doing this, to introduce the notion of the *right* action for an agent in given circumstances. I take it that in any form of direct consequentialism, and certainly in act-utilitarianism, the notion of the right action in given circumstances is a maximizing notion:[1] the right action is that which out of the actions available to the agent brings about or represents the highest degree of whatever it is the system in question regards as intrinsically valuable – in the central case, utilitarianism, this is of course happiness. In this argument, I shall confine myself to direct consequentialism, for which 'right action' is unqualifiedly a maximizing notion.

The notion of the right action as that which, of the possible

[1] Cf. Smart's definition, p. 45.

alternatives, maximizes the good (where this embraces, in unfavourable circumstances, minimizing the bad), is an objective notion in this sense, that it is perfectly possible for an agent to be ignorant or mistaken, and non-culpably ignorant or mistaken, about what is the right action in the circumstances. Thus the assessment by others of whether the agent did, in this sense, do the right thing, is not bounded by the agent's state of knowledge at the time, and the claim that he did the wrong thing is compatible with recognizing that he did as well as anyone in his state of knowledge could have done.[1] It might be suggested that, contrary to this, we have already imported the subjective conditions of action in speaking of the best of the actions *available to him*: if he is ignorant or misinformed, then the actions which might seem to us available to him were not in any real sense available. But this would be an exaggeration; the notion of availability imports some, but not all, kinds of subjective condition. Over and above the question of actions which, granted his situation and powers, were physically not available to him, we might perhaps add that a course of action was not really available to an agent if his historical, cultural or psychological situation was such that it could not possibly occur to him. But it is scarcely reasonable to extend the notion of unavailability to actions which merely did not occur to him; and surely absurd to extend it to actions which did occur to him, but where he was misinformed about their consequences.

If then an agent does the right thing, he does the best of the alternatives available to him (where that, again, embraces the least bad: we shall omit this rider from now on). Standardly, the action will be right in virtue of its causal properties, of maximally conducing to good states of affairs. Sometimes, however, the relation of the action to the good state of affairs may not be that of cause to effect – the good state

[1] In Smart's terminology, the 'rational thing': pp. 46–7.

of affairs may be constituted, or partly constituted, by the agent's doing that act (as when under utilitarianism he just enjoys doing it, and there is no project available to him more productive of happiness for him or anyone else).

Although this may be so under consequentialism, there seems to be an important difference between this situation and a situation of an action's being right for some non-consequentialist reason, as for instance under a Kantian morality. This difference might be brought out intuitively by saying that for the consequentialist, even a situation of this kind in which the action itself possesses intrinsic value is one in which the rightness of the act is derived from the goodness of a certain state of affairs – the act is right *because* the state of affairs which consists in its being done is better than any other state of affairs accessible to the agent; whereas for the non-consequentialist it is sometimes, at least, the other way round, and a state of affairs which is better than the alternatives is so because it consists of the right act being done. This intuitive description of the difference has something in it, but it needs to be made more precise.

We can take a step towards making it more precise, perhaps, in the following way. Suppose S is some particular concrete situation. Consider the statement, made about some particular agent

(1) In S, he did the right thing in doing A.

For consequentialists, (1) implies a statement of the form

(2) The state of affairs P is better than any other state of affairs accessible to him;

where a state of affairs being 'accessible' to an agent means that it is a state of affairs which is the consequence of, or is constituted by, his doing an act available to him (for that, see above); and P is a state of affairs accessible to him only in virtue of his doing A.[1]

---

[1] 'Only' here may seem a bit strong: but I take it that it is not an unreasonable demand on an account of his doing *the* right thing in S that his

Now in the exceptional case where it is just his doing *A* which carries the intrinsic value, we get for (2)

(3) The state of affairs which consists in his doing *A* is better than any other state of affairs accessible to him.

It was just the possibility of this sort of case which raised the difficulty of not being able to distinguish between a sophisticated consequentialism and non-consequentialism. The question thus is: if (3) is what we get for consequentialism in this sort of case, is it what a non-consequentialist would regard as implied by (1)? If so, we still cannot tell the difference between them. But the answer in fact seems to be 'no'.

There are two reasons for this. One reason is that a non-consequentialist, though he must inevitably be able to attach a sense to (1), does not have to be able to attach a sense to (3) at all, while the consequentialist, of course, attaches a sense to (1) only because he attaches a sense to (3). Although the non-consequentialist is concerned with right actions – such as the carrying out of promises – he may have no general way of comparing states of affairs from a moral point of view at all. Indeed, we shall see later and in greater depth than these schematic arguments allow, that the emphasis on the necessary comparability of situations is a peculiar feature of consequentialism in general, and of utilitarianism in particular.

A different kind of reason emerges if we suppose that the non-consequentialist does admit, in general, comparison between states of affairs. Thus, we might suppose that some non-consequentialist would consider it a better state of things in which more, rather than fewer, people kept their promises, and kept them for non-consequentialist reasons.

---

action is uniquely singled out from the alternatives. A further detail: one should strictly say, not that (1) implies a statement of the form (2), but that (1) implies *that there is* a true statement of that form.

Yet consistently with that he could accept, in a particular case, all of the following: that X would do the right thing only if he kept his promise; that keeping his promise would involve (or consist in) doing A; that several other people would, as a matter of fact, keep their promises (and for the right reasons) if and only if X did not do A. There are all sorts of situations in which this sort of thing would be true: thus it might be the case that an effect of X's doing A would be to provide some inducement to these others which would lead them to break promises which otherwise they would have kept. Thus a non-consequentialist can hold both that it is a better state of affairs in which more people keep their promises, and that the right thing for X to do is something which brings it about that fewer promises are kept. Moreover, it is very obvious what view of things goes with holding that. It is one in which, even though from some abstract point of view one state of affairs is better than another, it does not follow that a given agent should regard it as his business to bring it about, even though it is open to him to do so. More than that, it might be that he could not properly regard it as his business. If the goodness of the world were to consist in people's fulfilling their obligations, it would by no means follow that one of my obligations was to bring it about that other people kept their obligations.

Of course, no sane person could really believe that the goodness of the world just consisted in people keeping their obligations. But that is just an example, to illustrate the point that under non-consequentialism (3) does not, as one might expect, follow from (1). Thus even allowing some actions to have intrinsic value, we can still distinguish consequentialism. A consequentialist view, then, is one in which a statement of the form (2) follows from a statement of the form (1). A non-consequentialist view is one in which this is not so – not even when the (2)-statement takes the special form of (3).

This is not at all to say that the alternative to consequentialism is that one has to accept that there are some actions which one should always do, or again some which one should never do, *whatever the consequences*: this is a much stronger position than any involved, as I have defined the issues, in the denial of consequentialism. All that is involved, on the present account, in the denial of consequentialism, is that with respect to some type of action, there are some situations in which that would be the right thing to do, even though the state of affairs produced by one's doing that would be worse than some other state of affairs accessible to one. The claim that there is a type of action which is right *whatever the consequences* can be put by saying that with respect to some type of action, assumed as being adequately specified, then *whatever* the situation may (otherwise) be, that will be the right thing to do, *whatever* other state of affairs might be accessible to one, however much better it might be than the state of affairs produced by one's doing this action.

If that somewhat Moorean formulation has not hopelessly concealed the point, it will be seen that this second position – the *whatever the consequences* position – is very much stronger than the first, the mere rejection of consequentialism. It is perfectly consistent, and it might be thought a mark of sense, to believe, while not being a consequentialist, that there was no type of action which satisfied this second condition: that if an adequate (and non-question-begging) specification of a type of action has been given in advance, it is always possible to think of some situation in which the consequences of doing the action so specified would be so awful that it would be right to do something else.

Of course, one might think that there just *were* some types of action which satisfied this condition; though it seems to me obscure how one could have much faith in a list of such actions unless one supposed that it had supernatural warrant.

Alternatively, one might think that while logically there was a difference between the two positions, in social and psychological fact they came to much the same thing, since so soon (it might be claimed) as people give up thinking in terms of certain things being right or wrong whatever the consequences, they turn to thinking in purely consequential terms. This might be offered as a very general proposition about human thought, or (more plausibly) as a sociological proposition about certain situations of social change, in which utilitarianism (in particular) looks the only coherent alternative to a dilapidated set of values. At the level of language, it is worth noting that the use of the word '*absolute*' mirrors, and perhaps also assists, this association: the claim that no type of action is 'absolutely right' – leaving aside the sense in which it means that the rightness of anything depends on the value-system of a society (the confused doctrine of relativism) – can mean either that no type of action is right-whatever-its-consequences, or, alternatively, that 'it all depends on the consequences', that is, in each case the decision whether an action is right is determined by its consequences.

A particular sort of psychological connexion – or in an old-fashioned use of the term, a 'moral' connexion – between the two positions might be found in this. If people do not regard certain things as 'absolutely out', then they are prepared to start thinking about extreme situations in which what would otherwise be out might, exceptionally, be justified. They will, if they are to get clear about what they believe, be prepared to compare different extreme situations and ask what action would be justified in them. But once they have got used to that, their inhibitions about thinking of everything in consequential terms disappear: the difference between the extreme situations and the less extreme, presents itself no longer as a difference between the exceptional and the usual, but between the greater and the less –

and the consequential thoughts one was prepared to deploy in the greater it may seem quite irrational not to deploy in the less. *A fortiori*, someone might say: but he would have already had to complete this process to see it as a case of *a fortiori*.

One could regard this process of adaptation to consequentialism, moreover, not merely as a blank piece of psychological association, but as concealing a more elaborate structure of thought. One might have the idea that the *unthinkable* was itself a moral category; and in more than one way. It could be a feature of a man's moral outlook that he regarded certain courses of action as unthinkable, in the sense that he would not entertain the idea of doing them: and the witness to that might, in many cases, be that they simply would not come into his head. Entertaining certain alternatives, regarding them indeed as *alternatives*, is itself something that he regards as dishonourable or morally absurd. But, further, he might equally find it unacceptable to consider what to do in certain conceivable situations. Logically, or indeed empirically conceivable they may be, but they are not to him morally conceivable, meaning by that that their occurrence as situations presenting him with a choice would represent not a special problem in his moral world, but something that lay beyond its limits. For him, there are certain situations so monstrous that the idea that the processes of moral rationality could yield an answer in them is insane: they are situations which so transcend in enormity the human business of moral deliberation that from a moral point of view it cannot matter any more what happens. Equally, for him, to spend time thinking what one would decide if one were in such a situation is also insane, if not merely frivolous.

For such a man, and indeed for anyone who is prepared to take him seriously, the demand, in Herman Kahn's words, to *think the unthinkable* is not an unquestionable demand of rationality, set against a cowardly or inert refusal to follow out one's moral thoughts. Rationality he sees as a demand not merely on him, but on the situations in, and about, which he has to think; unless the environment reveals minimum sanity, it is insanity to carry the decorum of sanity into it. Consequentialist rationality, however, and in particular utilitarian rationality, has no such limitations: making the best of a bad job is one of its maxims, and it will have something to say even on the difference between massacring seven million, and massacring seven million and one.

There are other important questions about the idea of the morally unthinkable, which we cannot pursue here. Here we have been concerned with the role it might play in someone's connecting, by more than a mistake, the idea that there was nothing which was right whatever the consequences, and the different idea that everything depends on consequences. While someone might, in this way or another, move from one of those ideas to the other, it is very important that the two ideas are different: especially important in a world where we have lost traditional reasons for resisting the first idea, but have more than enough reasons for fearing the second.

3. Negative responsibility: and two examples

Although I have defined a state of affairs being *accessible* to an agent in terms of the actions which are *available* to him,[1] nevertheless it is the former notion which is really more important for consequentialism. Consequentialism is basically indifferent to whether a state of affairs consists in what I do, or is produced by what I do, where that notion is itself wide enough to include, for instance, situations in which other people do things which I have made them do, or allowed them to do, or encouraged them to do, or given them a chance to do. All that consequentialism is interested in is

[1] See last section, p. 87.

the idea of these doings being *consequences* of what I do, and that is a relation broad enough to include the relations just mentioned, and many others.

Just what the relation is, is a different question, and at least as obscure as the nature of its relative, cause and effect. It is not a question I shall try to pursue; I will rely on cases where I suppose that any consequentialist would be bound to regard the situations in question as consequences of what the agent does. There are cases where the supposed consequences stand in a rather remote relation to the action, which are sometimes difficult to assess from a practical point of view, but which raise no very interesting question for the present enquiry. The more interesting points about consequentialism lie rather elsewhere. There are certain situations in which the causation of the situation, the relation it has to what I do, is in no way remote or problematic in itself, and entirely justifies the claim that the situation is a consequence of what I do: for instance, it is quite clear, or reasonably clear, that if I do a certain thing, this situation will come about, and if I do not, it will not. So from a consequentialist point of view it goes into the calculation of consequences along with any other state of affairs accessible to me. Yet from some, at least, non-consequentialist points of view, there is a vital difference between some such situations and others: namely, that in some a vital link in the production of the eventual outcome is provided by *someone else's* doing something. But for consequentialism, all causal connexions are on the same level, and it makes no difference, so far as that goes, whether the causation of a given state of affairs lies through another agent, or not.

Correspondingly, there is no relevant difference which consists *just* in one state of affairs being brought about by me, without intervention of other agents, and another being brought about through the intervention of other agents; although some genuinely causal differences involving a difference of value may correspond to that (as when, for instance, the other agents derive pleasure or pain from the transaction), that kind of difference will already be included in the specification of the state of affairs to be produced. Granted that the states of affairs have been adequately described in causally and evaluatively relevant terms, it makes no further comprehensible difference who produces them. It is because consequentialism attaches value ultimately to states of affairs, and its concern is with what states of affairs the world contains, that it essentially involves the notion of *negative responsibility*: that if I am ever responsible for anything, then I must be just as much responsible for things that I allow or fail to prevent, as I am for things that I myself, in the more everyday restricted sense, bring about.[1] Those things also must enter my deliberations, as a responsible moral agent, on the same footing. What matters is what states of affairs the world contains, and so what matters with respect to a given action is what comes about if it is done, and what comes about if it is not done, and those are questions not intrinsically affected by the nature of the causal linkage, in particular by whether the outcome is partly produced by other agents.

The strong doctrine of negative responsibility flows directly from consequentialism's assignment of ultimate value to states of affairs. Looked at from another point of view, it can be seen also as a special application of something that is favoured in many moral outlooks not themselves consequentialist – something which, indeed, some thinkers have been disposed to regard as the essence of morality

[1] This is a fairly modest sense of 'responsibility', introduced merely by one's ability to reflect on, and decide, what one ought to do. This presumably escapes Smart's ban (p. 54) on the notion of 'the responsibility' as 'a piece of metaphysical nonsense' – his remarks seem to be concerned solely with situations of inter-personal blame. For the limitations of that, see below, section 6 (pp. 123 ff.).

itself: a principle of impartiality. Such a principle will claim that there can be no relevant difference from a moral point of view which consists just in the fact, not further explicable in general terms, that benefits or harms accrue to one person rather than to another – 'it's me' can never in itself be a morally comprehensible reason.[1] This principle, familiar with regard to the reception of harms and benefits, we can see consequentialism as extending to their production: from the moral point of view, there is no comprehensible difference which consists just in my bringing about a certain outcome rather than someone else's producing it. That the doctrine of negative responsibility represents in this way the extreme of impartiality, and abstracts from the identity of the agent, leaving just a locus of causal intervention in the world – that fact is not merely a surface paradox. It helps to explain why consequentialism can seem to some to express a more serious attitude than non-consequentialist views, why part of its appeal is to a certain kind of high-mindedness. Indeed, that is part of what is wrong with it.

For a lot of the time so far we have been operating at an exceedingly abstract level. This has been necessary in order to get clearer in general terms about the differences between consequentialist and other outlooks, an aim which is important if we want to know what features of them lead to what results for our thought. Now, however, let us look more concretely at two examples, to see what utilitarianism might say about them, what we might say about utilitarianism and, most importantly of all, what would be implied by certain ways of thinking about the situations. The examples are inevitably schematized, and they are open to the objection that they beg as many questions as they illuminate. There are two ways in particular in which examples in

[1] There is a tendency in some writers to suggest that it is not a comprehensible reason at all. But this, I suspect, is due to the overwhelming importance those writers ascribe to the moral point of view.

moral philosophy tend to beg important questions. One is that, as presented, they arbitrarily cut off and restrict the range of alternative courses of action – this objection might particularly be made against the first of my two examples. The second is that they inevitably present one with the situation as a going concern, and cut off questions about how the agent got into it, and correspondingly about moral considerations which might flow from that: this objection might perhaps specially arise with regard to the second of my two situations. These difficulties, however, just have to be accepted, and if anyone finds these examples cripplingly defective in this sort of respect, then he must in his own thought rework them in richer and less question-begging form. If he feels that no presentation of any imagined situation can ever be other than misleading in morality, and that there can never be any substitute for the concrete experienced complexity of actual moral situations, then this discussion, with him, must certainly grind to a halt: but then one may legitimately wonder whether every discussion with him about conduct will not grind to a halt, including any discussion about the actual situations, since discussion about how one would think and feel about situations some-what different from the actual (that is to say, situations to that extent imaginary) plays an important role in discussion of the actual.

(1) George, who has just taken his Ph.D. in chemistry, finds it extremely difficult to get a job. He is not very robust in health, which cuts down the number of jobs he might be able to do satisfactorily. His wife has to go out to work to keep them, which itself causes a great deal of strain, since they have small children and there are severe problems about looking after them. The results of all this, especially on the children, are damaging. An older chemist, who knows about this situation, says that he can get George a decently paid job in a certain laboratory, which pursues research into

chemical and biological warfare. George says that he cannot accept this, since he is opposed to chemical and biological warfare. The older man replies that he is not too keen on it himself, come to that, but after all George's refusal is not going to make the job or the laboratory go away; what is more, he happens to know that if George refuses the job, it will certainly go to a contemporary of George's who is not inhibited by any such scruples and is likely if appointed to push along the research with greater zeal than George would. Indeed, it is not merely concern for George and his family, but (to speak frankly and in confidence) some alarm about this other man's excess of zeal, which has led the older man to offer to use his influence to get George the job . . . George's wife, to whom he is deeply attached, has views (the details of which need not concern us) from which it follows that at least there is nothing particularly wrong with research into CBW. What should he do?

(2) Jim finds himself in the central square of a small South American town. Tied up against the wall are a row of twenty Indians, most terrified, a few defiant, in front of them several armed men in uniform. A heavy man in a sweat-stained khaki shirt turns out to be the captain in charge and, after a good deal of questioning of Jim which establishes that he got there by accident while on a botanical expedition, explains that the Indians are a random group of the inhabitants who, after recent acts of protest against the government, are just about to be killed to remind other possible protestors of the advantages of not protesting. However, since Jim is an honoured visitor from another land, the captain is happy to offer him a guest's privilege of killing one of the Indians himself. If Jim accepts, then as a special mark of the occasion, the other Indians will be let off. Of course, if Jim refuses, then there is no special occasion, and Pedro here will do what he was about to do when Jim arrived, and kill them all. Jim, with some desperate recollec-

tion of schoolboy fiction, wonders whether if he got hold of a gun, he could hold the captain, Pedro and the rest of the soldiers to threat, but it is quite clear from the set-up that nothing of that kind is going to work: any attempt at that sort of thing will mean that all the Indians will be killed, and himself. The men against the wall, and the other villagers, understand the situation, and are obviously begging him to accept. What should he do?

To these dilemmas, it seems to me that utilitarianism replies, in the first case, that George should accept the job, and in the second, that Jim should kill the Indian. Not only does utilitarianism give these answers but, if the situations are essentially as described and there are no further special factors, it regards them, it seems to me, as *obviously* the right answers. But many of us would certainly wonder whether, in (1), that could possibly be the right answer at all; and in the case of (2), even one who came to think that perhaps that was the answer, might well wonder whether it was obviously the answer. Nor is it just a question of the rightness or obviousness of these answers. It is also a question of what sort of considerations come into finding the answer. A feature of utilitarianism is that it cuts out a kind of consideration which for some others makes a difference to what they feel about such cases: a consideration involving the idea, as we might first and very simply put it, that each of us is specially responsible for what *he* does, rather than for what other people do. This is an idea closely connected with the value of integrity. It is often suspected that utilitarianism, at least in its direct forms, makes integrity as a value more or less unintelligible. I shall try to show that this suspicion is correct. Of course, even if that is correct, it would not necessarily follow that we should reject utilitarianism; perhaps, as utilitarians sometimes suggest, we should just forget about integrity, in favour of such things as a concern for the general good. However, if I am right, we cannot merely do that, since the reason why utilitarianism cannot understand integrity is that it cannot coherently describe the relations between a man's projects and his actions.

4. Two kinds of remoter effect

A lot of what we have to say about this question will be about the relations between my projects and other people's projects. But before we get on to that, we should first ask whether we are assuming too hastily what the utilitarian answers to the dilemmas will be. In terms of more direct effects of the possible decisions, there does not indeed seem much doubt about the answer in either case; but it might be said that in terms of more remote or less evident effects counterweights might be found to enter the utilitarian scales. Thus the effect on George of a decision to take the job might be invoked, or its effect on others who might know of his decision. The possibility of there being more beneficent labours in the future from which he might be barred or disqualified, might be mentioned; and so forth. Such effects – in particular, possible effects on the agent's character, and effects on the public at large – are often invoked by utilitarian writers dealing with problems about lying or promise-breaking, and some similar considerations might be invoked here.

There is one very general remark that is worth making about arguments of this sort. The certainty that attaches to these hypotheses about possible effects is usually pretty low; in some cases, indeed, the hypothesis invoked is so implausible that it would scarcely pass if it were not being used to deliver the respectable moral answer, as in the standard fantasy that one of the effects of one's telling a particular lie is to weaken the disposition of the world at large to tell the truth. The demands on the certainty or probability of these beliefs as beliefs about particular actions are much milder than they would be on beliefs favouring the unconventional course. It may be said that this is as it should be, since the presumption must be in favour of the conventional course: but that scarcely seems a *utilitarian* answer, unless utilitarianism has already taken off in the direction of not applying the consequences to the particular act at all.

Leaving aside that very general point, I want to consider now two types of effect that are often invoked by utilitarians, and which might be invoked in connexion with these imaginary cases. The attitude or tone involved in invoking these effects may sometimes seem peculiar; but that sort of peculiarity soon becomes familiar in utilitarian discussions, and indeed it can be something of an achievement to retain a sense of it.

First, there is the psychological effect on the agent. Our descriptions of these situations have not so far taken account of how George or Jim will be after they have taken the one course or the other; and it might be said that if they take the course which seemed at first the utilitarian one, the effects on them will be in fact bad enough and extensive enough to cancel out the initial utilitarian advantages of that course. Now there is one version of this effect in which, for a utilitarian, some confusion must be involved, namely that in which the agent feels bad, his subsequent conduct and relations are crippled and so on, *because he thinks that he has done the wrong thing* – for if the balance of outcomes was as it appeared to be *before* invoking this effect, then he has not (from the utilitarian point of view) done the wrong thing. So that version of the effect, for a rational and utilitarian agent, could not possibly make any difference to the assessment of right and wrong. However, perhaps he is not a thoroughly rational agent, and is disposed to have bad feelings, whichever he decided to do. Now such feelings, which are from a strictly utilitarian point of view irrational – nothing, a utilitarian can point out, is advanced by having them – cannot, consistently, have any great weight in a utilitarian calculation. I shall consider in a moment an argument to suggest that they should have no weight at all in it. But short of that, the utilitarian could reasonably say that such feelings should not be encouraged, even if we accept their existence, and that to give them a lot of weight is to encourage them. Or, at the very best, even if they are straightforwardly and without any discount to be put into the calculation, their weight must be small: they are after all (and at best) one man's feelings.

That consideration might seem to have particular force in Jim's case. In George's case, his feelings represent a larger proportion of what is to be weighed, and are more commensurate in character with other items in the calculation. In Jim's case, however, his feelings might seem to be of very little weight compared with other things that are at stake. There is a powerful and recognizable appeal that can be made on this point: as that a refusal by Jim to do what he has been invited to do would be a kind of self-indulgent squeamishness. That is an appeal which can be made by other than utilitarians – indeed, there are some uses of it which cannot be consistently made by utilitarians, as when it essentially involves the idea that there is something dishonourable about such self-indulgence. But in some versions it is a familiar, and it must be said a powerful, weapon of utilitarianism. One must be clear, though, about what it can and cannot accomplish. The most it can do, so far as I can see, is to invite one to consider how seriously, and for what reasons, one feels that what one is invited to do is (in these circumstances) wrong, and in particular, to consider that question from the utilitarian point of view. When the agent is not seeing the situation from a utilitarian point of view, the appeal cannot force him to do so; and if he does come round to seeing it from a utilitarian point of view, there is virtually nothing left for the appeal to do. If he does not see

it from a utilitarian point of view, he will not see his resis-
tance to the invitation, and the unpleasant feelings he
associates with accepting it, *just* as disagreeable experiences
of his; they figure rather as emotional expressions of a thought
that to accept would be wrong. He may be asked, as by the
appeal, to consider whether he is right, and indeed whether
he is fully serious, in thinking that. But the assertion of the
appeal, that he is being self-indulgently squeamish, will not
itself answer that question, or even help to answer it, since
it essentially tells him to regard his feelings just as unpleasant
experiences of his, and he cannot, by doing that, answer the
question they pose when they are precisely not so regarded,
but are regarded as indications[1] of what he thinks is right and
wrong. If he does come round fully to the utilitarian point
of view then of course he will regard these feelings just as
unpleasant experiences of his. And once Jim – at least – has
come to see them in that light, there is nothing left for the
appeal to do, since *of course* his feelings, so regarded, are of
virtually no weight at all in relation to the other things at
stake. The 'squeamishness' appeal is not an argument which
adds in a hitherto neglected consideration. Rather, it is an
invitation to consider the situation, and one's own feelings,
from a utilitarian point of view.

The reason why the squeamishness appeal can be very
unsettling, and one can be unnerved by the suggestion of
self-indulgence in going against utilitarian considerations, is
not that we are utilitarians who are uncertain what utilitarian
value to attach to our moral feelings, but that we are par-
tially at least not utilitarians, and cannot regard our moral
feelings merely as objects of utilitarian value. Because our
moral relation to the world is partly given by such feelings,
and by a sense of what we can or cannot 'live with', to come

---

[1] On the non-cognitivist meta-ethic in terms of which Smart presents
his utilitarianism, the term 'indications' here would represent an
understatement.

to regard those feelings from a purely utilitarian point of view, that is to say, as happenings outside one's moral self, is to lose a sense of one's moral identity; to lose, in the most literal way, one's integrity. At this point utilitarianism alienates one from one's moral feelings; we shall see a little later how, more basically, it alienates one from one's actions as well.

If, then, one is really going to regard one's feelings from a strictly utilitarian point of view, Jim should give very little weight at all to his; it seems almost indecent, in fact, once one has taken that point of view, to suppose that he should give any at all. In George's case one might feel that things were slightly different. It is interesting, though, that one reason why one might think that – namely that one person principally affected is his wife – is very dubiously available to a utilitarian. George's wife has some reason to be interested in George's integrity and his sense of it; the Indians, quite properly, have no interest in Jim's. But it is not at all clear how utilitarianism would describe that difference.

There is an argument, and a strong one, that a strict utilitarian should give not merely small extra weight, in calculations of right and wrong, to feelings of this kind, but that he should give absolutely no weight to them at all. This is based on the point, which we have already seen, that if a course of action is, before taking these sorts of feelings into account, utilitarianly preferable, then bad feelings about that kind of action will be from a utilitarian point of view irrational. Now it might be thought that even if that is so, it would not mean that in a utilitarian calculation such feelings should not be taken into account; it is after all a well-known boast of utilitarianism that it is a realistic outlook which seeks the best in the world as it is, and takes any form of happiness or unhappiness into account. While a utilitarian will no doubt seek to diminish the incidence of feelings which are utilitarianly irrational – or at least of disagreeable feelings which are so – he might be expected to take them into account while they exist. This is without doubt classical utilitarian doctrine, but there is good reason to think that utilitarianism cannot stick to it without embracing results which are startlingly unacceptable and perhaps self-defeating.

Suppose that there is in a certain society a racial minority. Considering merely the ordinary interests of the other citizens, as opposed to their sentiments, this minority does no particular harm; we may suppose that it does not confer any very great benefits either. Its presence is in those terms neutral or mildly beneficial. However, the other citizens have such prejudices that they find the sight of this group, even the knowledge of its presence, very disagreeable. Proposals are made for removing in some way this minority. If we assume various quite plausible things (as that programmes to change the majority sentiment are likely to be protracted and ineffective) then even if the removal would be unpleasant for the minority, a utilitarian calculation might well end up favouring this step, especially if the minority were a rather small minority and the majority were very severely prejudiced, that is to say, were made very severely uncomfortable by the presence of the minority.

A utilitarian might find that conclusion embarrassing; and not merely because of its nature, but because of the grounds on which it is reached. While a utilitarian might be expected to take into account certain other sorts of consequences of the prejudice, as that a majority prejudice is likely to be displayed in conduct disagreeable to the minority, and so forth, he might be made to wonder whether the unpleasant experiences of the prejudiced people should be allowed, *merely as such*, to count. If he does count them, merely as such, then he has once more separated himself from a body of ordinary moral thought which he might have hoped to accommodate; he may also have started on the path of defeating his own view of things. For one feature of these sentiments is that they are from the utilitarian point of view itself irrational, and a thoroughly utilitarian person would either not have them, or if he found that he did tend to have them, would himself seek to discount them. Since the sentiments in question are such that a rational utilitarian would discount them in himself, it is reasonable to suppose that he should discount them in his calculations about society; it does seem quite unreasonable for him to give just as much weight to feelings – considered just in themselves, one must recall, as experiences of those that have them – which are essentially based on views which are from a utilitarian point of view irrational, as to those which accord with utilitarian principles. Granted this idea, it seems reasonable for him to rejoin a body of moral thought in other respects congenial to him, and discount those sentiments, just considered in themselves, totally, on the principle that no pains or discomforts are to count in the utilitarian sum which their subjects have just because they hold views which are by utilitarian standards irrational. But if he accepts that, then in the cases we are at present considering no extra weight at all can be put in for bad feelings of George or Jim about their choices, if those choices are, leaving out those feelings, on the first round utilitarianly rational.

The psychological effect on the agent was the first of two general effects considered by utilitarians, which had to be discussed. The second is in general a more substantial item, but it need not take so long, since it is both clearer and has little application to the present cases. This is the *precedent effect*. As Burke rightly emphasized, this effect can be important: that one morally *can* do what someone has actually done, is a psychologically effective principle, if not a deontically valid one. For the effect to operate, obviously some conditions must hold on the publicity of the act and on such things as the status of the agent (such considerations weighed importantly with Sir Thomas More); what these may be will vary evidently with circumstances.

In order for the precedent effect to make a difference to a utilitarian calculation, it must be based upon a confusion. For suppose that there is an act which would be the best in the circumstances, except that doing it will encourage by precedent other people to do things which will not be the best things to do. Then the situation of those other people must be relevantly different from that of the original agent; if it were not, then in doing the same as what would be the best course for the original agent, they would necessarily do the best thing themselves. But if the situations are in this way relevantly different, it must be a confused perception which takes the first situation, and the agent's course in it, as an adequate precedent for the second.

However, the fact that the precedent effect, if it really makes a difference, is in this sense based on a confusion, does not mean that it is not perfectly real, nor that it is to be discounted: social effects are by their nature confused in this sort of way. What it does emphasize is that calculations of the precedent effect have got to be realistic, involving considerations of how people are actually likely to be influenced. In the present examples, however, it is very implausible to think that the precedent effect could be invoked to make any difference to the calculation. Jim's case is extraordinary enough, and it is hard to imagine who the recipients of the effect might be supposed to be; while George is not in a sufficiently public situation or role for the question to arise in that form, and in any case one might suppose that the motivations of others on such an issue were quite likely to be fixed one way or another already.

No appeal, then, to these other effects is going to make a difference to what the utilitarian will decide about our examples. Let us now look more closely at the structure of those decisions.

5. Integrity

The situations have in common that if the agent does not do a certain disagreeable thing, someone else will, and in Jim's situation at least the result, the state of affairs after the other man has acted, if he does, will be worse than after Jim has acted, if Jim does. The same, on a smaller scale, is true of George's case. I have already suggested that it is inherent in consequentialism that it offers a strong doctrine of negative responsibility: if I know that if I do X, O_1 will eventuate, and if I refrain from doing X, O_2 will, and that O_2 is worse than O_1, then I am responsible for O_2 if I refrain voluntarily from doing X. 'You could have prevented it', as will be said, and truly, to Jim, if he refuses, by the relatives of the other Indians. (I shall leave the important question, which is to the side of the present issue, of the obligations, if any, that nest round the word 'know': how far does one, under utilitarianism, have to research into the possibilities of maximally beneficent action, including prevention?)

In the present cases, the situation of O_2 includes another agent bringing about results worse than O_1. So far as O_2 has been identified up to this point – merely as the worse outcome which will eventuate if I refrain from doing X – we might equally have said that what that other brings about is O_2; but that would be to underdescribe the situation. For what occurs if Jim refrains from action is not solely twenty Indians dead, but *Pedro's killing twenty Indians*, and that is not a result which Pedro brings about, though the death of the Indians is. We can say: what one does is not included in the outcome of what one does, while what another does can be included in the outcome of what one does. For that to be so, as the terms are now being used, only a very weak condition has to be satisfied: for Pedro's killing the Indians to be the outcome of Jim's refusal, it only has to be causally true that if Jim had not refused, Pedro would not have done it.

That may be enough for us to speak, in some sense, of Jim's responsibility for that outcome, if it occurs; but it is certainly not enough, it is worth noticing, for us to speak of Jim's *making* those things happen. For granted this way of their coming about, he could have made them happen only by making Pedro shoot, and there is no acceptable sense in which his refusal makes Pedro shoot. If the captain had said on Jim's refusal, 'you leave me with no alternative', he would have been lying, like most who use that phrase. While the deaths, and the killing, may be the outcome of Jim's refusal, it is misleading to think, in such a case, of Jim having an *effect* on the world through the medium (as it happens) of Pedro's acts; for this is to leave Pedro out of the picture in his essential role of one who has intentions and projects, projects for realizing which Jim's refusal would leave an opportunity. Instead of thinking in terms of supposed effects of Jim's projects on Pedro, it is more revealing to think in terms of the effects of Pedro's projects on Jim's decision. This is the direction from which I want to criticize the notion of negative responsibility.

There are of course other ways in which this notion can be criticized. Many have hoped to discredit it by insisting on the basic moral relevance of the distinction between action and inaction, between intervening and letting things take their course. The distinction is certainly of great moral significance, and indeed it is not easy to think of any moral outlook which could get along without making some use of it. But it is unclear, both in itself and in its moral applications, and the unclarities are of a kind which precisely cause it to give way when, in very difficult cases, weight has to be put on it. There is much to be said in this area, but I doubt whether the sort of dilemma we are considering is going to be resolved by a simple use of this distinction. Again, the issue of negative responsibility can be pressed on the question of how limits are to be placed on one's apparently

E

boundless obligation, implied by utilitarianism, to improve the world. Some answers are needed to that, too – and answers which stop short of relapsing into the bad faith of supposing that one's responsibilities could be adequately characterized just by appeal to one's roles.[1] But, once again, while that is a real question, it cannot be brought to bear directly on the present kind of case, since it is hard to think of anyone supposing that in Jim's case it would be an adequate response for him to say that it was none of his business.

What projects does a utilitarian agent have? As a utilitarian, he has the general project of bringing about maximally desirable outcomes; how he is to do this at any given moment is a question of what causal levers, so to speak, are at that moment within reach. The desirable outcomes, however, do not just consist of agents carrying out *that* project; there must be other more basic or lower-order projects which he and other agents have, and the desirable outcomes are going to consist, in part, of the maximally harmonious realization of those projects ('in part', because one component of a utilitarianly desirable outcome may be the occurrence of agreeable experiences which are not the satisfaction of anybody's projects). Unless there were first-order projects, the general utilitarian project would have nothing to work on, and would be vacuous. What do the more basic or lower-order projects comprise? Many will be the obvious kinds of desires for things for oneself, one's family, one's friends, including basic necessities of life, and in more relaxed circumstances, objects of taste. Or there may be pursuits and interests of an intellectual, cultural or creative character. I introduce those as a separate class not because the objects of them lie in a separate class, and provide – as some utilitarians, in their churchy way, are fond of saying – 'higher' pleasures. I introduce them separately because the agent's identification

[1] For some remarks bearing on this, see *Morality*, the section on 'Goodness and roles', and Cohen's article there cited.

with them may be of a different order. It does not have to be: cultural and aesthetic interests just belong, for many, along with any other taste; but some people's commitment to these kinds of interests just is at once more thoroughgoing and serious than their pursuit of various objects of taste, while it is more individual and permeated with character than the desire for the necessities of life.

Beyond these, someone may have projects connected with his support of some cause: Zionism, for instance, or the abolition of chemical and biological warfare. Or there may be projects which flow from some more general disposition towards human conduct and character, such as a hatred of injustice, or of cruelty, or of killing.

It may be said that this last sort of disposition and its associated project do not count as (logically) 'lower-order' relative to the higher-order project of maximizing desirable outcomes; rather, it may be said, it is itself a 'higher-order' project. The vital question is not, however, how it is to be classified, but whether it and similar projects are to count among the projects whose satisfaction is to be included in the maximizing sum, and, correspondingly, as contributing to the agent's happiness. If the utilitarian says 'no' to that, then he is almost certainly committed to a version of utilitarianism as absurdly superficial and shallow as Benthamite versions have often been accused of being. For this project will be discounted, presumably, on the ground that it involves, in the specification of its object, the mention of other people's happiness or interests: thus it is the kind of project which (unlike the pursuit of food for myself) presupposes a reference to other people's projects. But that criterion would eliminate any desire at all which was not blankly and in the most straightforward sense egoistic.[1] Thus we should be reduced

[1] On the subject of egoistic and non-egoistic desires, see 'Egoism and altruism', in *Problems of the Self* (Cambridge University Press, London, 1973).

to frankly egoistic first-order projects, and – for all essential purposes – the one second-order utilitarian project of maximally satisfying first-order projects. Utilitarianism has a tendency to slide in this direction, and to leave a vast hole in the range of human desires, between egoistic inclinations and necessities at one end, and impersonally benevolent happiness-management at the other. But the utilitarianism which has to leave this hole is the most primitive form, which offers a quite rudimentary account of desire. Modern versions of the theory are supposed to be neutral with regard to what sorts of things make people happy or what their projects are. Utilitarianism would do well then to acknowledge the evident fact that among the things that make people happy is not only making other people happy, but being taken up or involved in any of a vast range of projects, or – if we waive the evangelical and moralizing associations of the word – commitments. One can be committed to such things as a person, a cause, an institution, a career, one's own genius, or the pursuit of danger.

Now none of these is itself the *pursuit of happiness*: by an exceedingly ancient platitude, it is not at all clear that there could be anything which was just that, or at least anything that had the slightest chance of being successful. Happiness, rather, requires being involved in, or at least content with, something else.[1] It is not impossible for utilitarianism to accept that point: it does not have to be saddled with a naïve and absurd philosophy of mind about the relation between desire and happiness. What it does have to say is that if such

[1] This does not imply that there is no such thing as the project of pursuing pleasure. Some writers who have correctly resisted the view that all desires are desires for pleasure, have given an account of pleasure so thoroughly adverbial as to leave it quite unclear how there could be a distinctively hedonist way of life at all. Some room has to be left for that, though there are important difficulties both in defining it and living it. Thus (particularly in the case of the very rich) it often has highly ritual aspects, apparently part of a strategy to counter boredom.

commitments are worth while, then pursuing the projects that flow from them, and realizing some of those projects, will make the person for whom they are worth while, happy. It may be that to claim that is still wrong: it may well be that a commitment can make sense to a man (can make sense of his life) without his supposing that it will make him *happy*.[1] But that is not the present point; let us grant to utilitarianism that all worthwhile human projects must conduce, one way or another, to happiness. The point is that even if that is true, it does not follow, nor could it possibly be true, that those projects are themselves projects of pursuing happiness. One has to believe in, or at least want, or quite minimally, be content with, other things, for there to be anywhere that happiness can come from.

Utilitarianism, then, should be willing to agree that its general aim of maximizing happiness does not imply that what everyone is doing is just pursuing happiness. On the contrary, people have to be pursuing other things. What those other things may be, utilitarianism, sticking to its professed empirical stance, should be prepared just to find out. No doubt some possible projects it will want to discourage, on the grounds that their being pursued involves a negative balance of happiness to others: though even there, the unblinking accountant's eye of the strict utilitarian will have something to put in the positive column, the satisfactions of the destructive agent. Beyond that, there will be a vast variety of generally beneficent or at least harmless projects; and some no doubt, will take the form not just of tastes or fancies, but of what I have called 'commitments'. It may even be that the utilitarian researcher will find that many of those with commitments, who have really identified themselves with objects outside themselves, who are thoroughly involved with other persons, or institutions, or activities or

[1] For some remarks on this possibility, see *Morality*, section on 'What is morality about?'

causes, are actually happier than those whose projects and wants are not like that. If so, that is an important piece of utilitarian empirical lore.

When I say 'happier' here, I have in mind the sort of consideration which any utilitarian would be committed to accepting: as for instance that such people are less likely to have a break-down or commit suicide. Of course that is not all that is actually involved, but the point in this argument is to use to the maximum degree utilitarian notions, in order to locate a breaking point in utilitarian thought. In appealing to this strictly utilitarian notion, I am being more consistent with utilitarianism than Smart is. In his struggles with the problem of the brain-electrode man, Smart (p. 22) commends the idea that 'happy' is a partly evaluative term, in the sense that we call 'happiness' those kinds of satisfaction which, as things are, we approve of. But *by what standard* is this surplus element of approval supposed, from a utilitarian point of view, to be allocated? There is no source for it, on a strictly utilitarian view, except further degrees of satisfaction, but there are none of those available, or the problem would not arise. Nor does it help to appeal to the fact that we dislike in prospect things which we like when we get there, for from a utilitarian point of view it would seem that the original dislike was merely irrational or based on an error. Smart's argument at this point seems to be embarrassed by a well-known utilitarian uneasiness, which comes from a feeling that it is not respectable to ignore the 'deep', while not having anywhere left in human life to locate it.[1]

Let us now go back to the agent as utilitarian, and his higher-order project of maximizing desirable outcomes. At this level, he is committed only to that: what the outcome will actually consist of will depend entirely on the facts, on

[1] One of many resemblances in spirit between utilitarianism and high-minded evangelical Christianity.

what persons with what projects and what potential satisfactions there are within calculable reach of the causal levers near which he finds himself. His own substantial projects and commitments come into it, but only as one lot among others – they potentially provide one set of satisfactions among those which he may be able to assist from where he happens to be. He is the agent of the satisfaction system who happens to be at a particular point at a particular time: in Jim's case, our man in South America. His own decisions as a utilitarian agent are a function of all the satisfactions which he can affect from where he is: and this means that the projects of others, to an indeterminately great extent, determine his decision.

This may be so either positively or negatively. It will be so positively if agents within the causal field of his decision have projects which are at any rate harmless, and so should be assisted. It will equally be so, but negatively, if there is an agent within the causal field whose projects are harmful, and have to be frustrated to maximize desirable outcomes. So it is with Jim and the soldier Pedro. On the utilitarian view, the undesirable projects of other people as much determine, in this negative way, one's decisions as the desirable ones do positively: if those people were not there, or had different projects, the causal nexus would be different, and it is the actual state of the causal nexus which determines the decision. The determination to an indefinite degree of my decisions by other people's projects is just another aspect of my unlimited responsibility to act for the best in a causal framework formed to a considerable extent by their projects.

The decision so determined is, for utilitarianism, the right decision. But what if it conflicts with some project of mine? This, the utilitarian will say, has already been dealt with: the satisfaction to you of fulfilling your project, and any satisfactions to others of your so doing, have already been through the calculating device and have been found inadequate. Now in the case of many sorts of projects, that is a perfectly reasonable sort of answer. But in the case of projects of the sort I have called 'commitments', those with which one is more deeply and extensively involved and identified, this cannot just by itself be an adequate answer, and there may be no adequate answer at all. For, to take the extreme sort of case, how can a man, as a utilitarian agent, come to regard as one satisfaction among others, and a dispensable one, a project or attitude round which he has built his life, just because someone else's projects have so structured the causal scene that that is how the utilitarian sum comes out?

The point here is not, as utilitarians may hasten to say, that if the project or attitude is that central to his life, then to abandon it will be very disagreeable to him and great loss of utility will be involved. I have already argued in section 4 that it is not like that; on the contrary, once he is prepared to look at it like that, the argument in any serious case is over anyway. The point is that he is identified with his actions as flowing from projects and attitudes which in some cases he takes seriously at the deepest level, as what his life is about (or, in some cases, this section of his life – seriousness is not necessarily the same as persistence). It is absurd to demand of such a man, when the sums come in from the utility network which the projects of others have in part determined, that he should just step aside from his own project and decision and acknowledge the decision which utilitarian calculation requires. It is to alienate him in a real sense from his actions and the source of his action in his own convictions. It is to make him into a channel between the input of everyone's projects, including his own, and an output of optimific decision; but this is to neglect the extent to which *his* actions and *his* decisions have to be seen as the actions and decisions which flow from the projects and attitudes with which he is most closely identified. It is thus, in the most literal sense, an attack on his integrity.[1]

These sorts of considerations do not in themselves give solutions to practical dilemmas such as those provided by our examples; but I hope they help to provide other ways of thinking about them. In fact, it is not hard to see that in George's case, viewed from this perspective, the utilitarian solution would be wrong. Jim's case is different, and harder. But if (as I suppose) the utilitarian is probably right in this case, that is not to be found out just by asking the utilitarian's questions. Discussions of it – and I am not going to try to carry it further here – will have to take seriously the distinction between my killing someone, and its coming about because of what I do that someone else kills them: a distinction based, not so much on the distinction between action and inaction, as on the distinction between my projects and someone else's projects. At least it will have to start by taking that seriously, as utilitarianism does not; but then it will have to build out from there by asking why that distinction seems to have less, or a different, force in this case than it has in George's. One question here would be how far one's powerful objection to killing people just is, in fact, an application of a powerful objection to their being killed. Another dimension of that is the issue of how much it matters that the people at risk are actual, and there, as opposed to hypothetical, or future, or merely elsewhere.[2]

[1] Interestingly related to these notions is the Socratic idea that courage is a virtue particularly connected with keeping a clear sense of what one regards as most important. They also centrally raise questions about the value of pride. Humility, as something beyond the real demand of correct self-appraisal, was specially a Christian virtue because it involved subservience to God. In a secular context it can only represent subservience to other men and their projects.

[2] For a more general discussion of this issue see Charles Fried, *An Anatomy of Values* (Harvard University Press, Cambridge, Mass., 1970), Part Three.

There are many other considerations that could come into such a question, but the immediate point of all this is to draw one particular contrast with utilitarianism: that to reach a grounded decision in such a case should not be regarded as a matter of just discounting one's reactions, impulses and deeply held projects in the face of the pattern of utilities, nor yet merely adding them in – but in the first instance of trying to understand them.

Of course, time and circumstances are unlikely to make a grounded decision, in Jim's case at least, possible. It might not even be decent. Instead of thinking in a rational and systematic way either about utilities or about the value of human life, the relevance of the people at risk being present, and so forth, the presence of the people at risk may just have its effect. The significance of the immediate should not be underestimated. Philosophers, not only utilitarian ones, repeatedly urge one to view the world *sub specie aeternitatis*,[1] but for most human purposes that is not a good *species* to view it under. If we are not agents of the universal satisfaction system, we are not primarily janitors of any system of values, even our own: very often, we just act, as a possibly confused result of the situation in which we are engaged. That, I suspect, is very often an exceedingly good thing. To what extent utilitarians regard it as a good thing is an obscure question. To that sort of question I now turn.

6. The indirect pursuit of utility

Smart's defence is devoted to act-utilitarianism, which (taking for granted the complications which we have pursued in section 2) stands as the view that the rightness of any particular act depends on the goodness of its conse-

[1] Cf. Smart, p. 63.

quences. This is what I called in section 1 *direct* consequentialism; where the goodness of the consequences is cashed in terms of happiness, we can speak of direct utilitarianism. What is direct utilitarianism contrasted with? We cannot just say that direct utilitarianism considers only the utility of actions, while indirect utilitarianism, by contrast, is prepared to consider the utility of things other than actions, such as rules, institutions and dispositions of character. Clearly the act-utilitarian must be prepared to consider the utility of anything: his aim is to maximize utility, and anything, of whatever type, whose existence, introduction or whatever has effects on the amount of satisfaction in the world must be a candidate for assessment by the utilitarian standard. Thus if there *is* anything which has got a utility which cannot be counted in terms of the utility of particular acts, then the utility of that thing as well must be of interest to the direct utilitarian.

Here someone might say that there was nothing which had a utility which could not be counted in terms of the utility of particular acts. If institutions or rules or dispositions of character possess utility, then they possess it in terms of the acts which they variously encourage, license, enjoin or lead to. To take, in particular, the case of a rule: consider two states of society, one in which a given rule obtains, and another in which it does not. If there is a difference of utility between them which relates to this difference, then (it may be said) there must be a difference in the set of acts which occur in the two states, to which that difference in utility must be traceable. Different acts are done as a result of the rule obtaining. There have to be some such acts, on anyone's view, if we are to say that the rule *obtains* at all; other acts come into it in terms of rules being inculcated, thought of, brought up as matters of reproach, and in many other ways. In the end, it may be said, the total utility effect of a rule's obtaining must be cashable in terms of the effects of acts.

Let us call this, in a barbarous phrase, the 'act-adequacy premiss'.[1]

But if that premiss is right, then it becomes unclear what the difference between direct and indirect utilitarianism is. For so long at least as we regard utilitarianism as a system of *total assessment* – as providing an answer, basically, to the question 'how is the world going?' – then, on the present argument, it looks as though anything that anybody else can do, the direct utilitarian can do at least as well. If all the other candidates for utilitarian assessment, such as rules, can have their differential utility cashed in terms of acts, then the direct utilitarian can assess their contribution to the world as well as he can assess acts which are not particularly associated with rules. Whether the total utility of the social state in which the rule obtains is greater or less, measured by these means, than that of a state in which it does not obtain, then appears to be a totally empirical question, and it can scarcely be that the difference between direct and indirect utilitarianism consists just in giving different answers to that.

Suppose, on the other hand, that the act-adequacy premiss is false, and that there is, as it were, a surplus causal effect of the rule's obtaining which cannot be expressed in terms of the effects of acts. Then indeed, the direct utilitarian will not be able to capture all differences of utility just by counting the utility of acts. But equally, if that is so, then he must, from a utilitarian point of view, be quite irrational in insisting on so doing. As a utilitarian, as we said just now, he must be concerned with the utility in the world – and if utility can leak into or out of the world by channels which do not run totally through acts, then he would be mad to take no account of them.

As systems of total assessment then, it looks so far as though

[1] I shall not try to fill in any more determinate content for this premiss; its role in the following arguments is of an essentially formal character.

either there really is no difference between direct and indirect utilitarianism, in the sense that the direct utilitarian can also take into account the effects of such things as rules, and it is just an empirical question what the effects are; or else there is a difference, and direct utilitarianism must, in terms of the overall aims of utilitarianism, be irrational, simply because it would be ignoring important sources of utility. Thus a large question seems to have been rather rapidly short-circuited. The reason for this is that we have started too far out, as it were, by comparing the two outlooks *as systems of total assessment*, and by asking whether, as such systems, they were concerned with anything but acts. Rather, we have to start by asking, to the extent that they are both concerned with acts, *how* they are each concerned with them.

The place to start, then, is back with the assessment of acts themselves. Thus, as we said at the beginning, direct utilitarianism regards that act as right which has the best consequences. So indirect utilitarianism may be expected to deny this, and to hold that some acts are right even though they are not utility-maximizing – for instance, because they are done in accordance with a rule which is utilitarianly valuable. Another version might be that an act could be right just because it was the expression of a character-disposition, the obtaining of which in society is utilitarianly valuable. Thus the difference might be captured in some such way, at the level of the assessment of particular acts. We must remember, however, that it is precisely with regard to the rightness of the acts, and not necessarily elsewhere in the contrast just sketched, that the difference can be captured. Thus if we ask the indirect utilitarian "What does the rightness of acts consist in?" we shall get an answer with which the direct utilitarian will to a certain extent disagree; and conversely. But if we ask either of them "In what does the value of rules, traits of character, etc., consist?", we shall not necessarily get different answers. For if the indirect utilitarian accepts what I called earlier the 'act-adequacy premiss' – and there is no inconsistency in his doing so – then he will reply "in the utility of the acts that follow on their existence", which is the answer that the direct utilitarian will give as well.

Not only can they agree on that, under the act-adequacy assumption, but they can agree importantly on its interpretation. Thus, to confine ourselves to the case of rules, they can agree, if they are sensible, that the utility of acts that follow on the obtaining of a rule is not to be equated with the utility of acts that consist in obeying the rule.[1] If the rule actually *obtains* in society, as opposed to having merely been promulgated, e.g. from some legal source, then we can say – by definition, indeed – that a good number of acts that are performed because it exists must be acts of obedience to it. But very many other acts, of many different kinds, are performed because a rule exists. Some of them we touched on earlier; they range from acts involved in teaching it to acts involved in avoiding detection for breaking it, and all make their contribution to the overall utility of its obtaining. To equate the utility of a rule's obtaining with the utility of its being followed is not the mark of any utilitarian doctrine, direct or indirect – it is just a sign of simple-mindedness.

Thus the distinction has turned out to centre on the rightness or wrongness of particular acts. But now the question arises of how the distinction, so set up, is to be used, and of what follows from particular acts being right or wrong for these different reasons. In particular, I shall ask these questions of Smart; other utilitarians, perhaps of more cognitivist outlook, may give different answers, but to

---

[1] Cf. Lyons's distinction between 'acceptance-utility' and 'following-utility'. *The Forms and Limits of Utilitarianism* (Oxford University Press, London, 1965), pp. 137 ff. Further distinctions are needed when there is question of formally adopting or promulgating a rule – thus it may not be obeyed at all. But these need not concern us here.

some extent these problems will arise with any current version of utilitarianism. On Smart's view, one thing certainly is *not* meant by saying that an act is right if it maximizes utility – namely, that if the act maximizes utility, then it will be right to announce to the agent himself, or to anyone else, that the act is right. For any such announcements must fall under the provision that he makes about praise and blame,[1] where the only consideration is the effectiveness or utility of the utterance, and that does not, as he several times reminds us, necessarily come to the same thing as the utility of the act which the utterance relates to. Thus he encourages the patient utilitarian faced with the magical society to think it better to commend and blame acts by the local standard rather than a utilitarian one, since confusion and disutility are likely to follow from an ill-considered dash by the natives to accommodate themselves to the utterances of this influential commentator.[2]

Smart's causal theory of moral comment has two familiar disadvantages. One is that, as a practice, it essentially lacks openness – that is to say, it is not possible for it to be openly known in the society what this practice is. If it were known, then it would in some part cease to work, since one important dimension, at least, by which moral comment can be efficacious is by those who receive it not thinking in terms of its being efficacious or not, but in terms of whether it is justified. It is a very evident fact that blame has a decreasing, or a counter-productive, effect if it is handed out in ways which its objects perceive as unfair. In regarding it as fair or not, its objects cannot merely be considering whether it will work or not. Thus if those who administer the blame, or some smaller class of knowing utilitarians standing behind those who administer it, do in effect think of the question of fairness as fundamentally the same as the question of efficacy,

[1] P. 53 al.
[2] Smart, p. 50.

then there has to be disingenuousness between them and the others, and the institution has to lack openness, in the sense that it will not work as an institution unless there is widespread ignorance about its real nature. This lack of openness, a notable feature of the arrangements which Smart proposes, I shall come back to in section 7.

The second weakness of the causal theory of moral comment is that it makes it very difficult to make sense of a man's view of his own conduct; particularly if he himself believes the causal theory, since then the lack of openness I have mentioned stands between the man and himself – it is hard to see how he can blame himself if he knows what he is doing in doing that. Now utilitarians in fact are not very keen on people blaming themselves, which they see as an unproductive activity: not to cry over spilt milk figures prominently among utilitarian proverbial injunctions (and carries the characteristically utilitarian thought that anything you might want to cry over is, like milk, replaceable). Rather, they are concerned with practical future effects, and the question of what is the right thing to do focusses essentially on the situation of decision: the central question is not, "did he (or I) do the right thing?" but "what is the right thing to do?". This emphasis on the practical decision-making aspect of moral thought is of course not peculiar to utilitarianism, but it is not surprising that utilitarianism should particularly emphasize it.

If the central question is the practical question of what is the right thing to do, the problem now is, what distinctive contribution to understanding that question and answering it does the direct utilitarian give us? He tells us that the answer to the question "what is the right thing to do?" is to be found in that act which has the best consequences. But it seems difficult to put that to any use in this connexion, except by taking it to imply the following: that the correct question to ask, if asking what is the right thing to do, is what act will have the best consequences. But the moment that has been accepted, we lose a distinction on which Smart, following Sidgwick, lays great weight – that between justification and motivation.

Smart makes much of this distinction, to reject the immediately calculative aspect of utilitarianism, and to commend such things as spontaneity[1], and he even is prepared to consider, though he rejects, Moore's idea that an act-utilitarian might never act in the spirit of an act- utilitarian.[2] But now, if our argument is right, it looks as though Smart has no room, or at least very little room, in which to make these manoeuvres. For we have tracked down the distinction between direct utilitarianism and other sorts of utilitarianism to a difference about what acts are right; and we have located the significance of that question, for a utilitarian, in the situation of decision; and we have found no alternative to taking its significance in that situation as a matter of the correct question to ask oneself; and that makes it a matter of motivation, of what people should think about in deciding what to do. So if Smart wishes to sustain a distinctively direct utilitarian position, then he cannot also use some of the devices of indirect utilitarianism to take the edge off it.

There is one area in which Smart himself seems happy to accept that point, namely with regard to rules. He says that if a utilitarian agent perceives that in particular circumstances the course with the best consequences all round consists in breaking the rule, then it would be 'rule-worship' not to do so; and that a utilitarian should regard rules as 'rules of thumb'[3]. I interpret this in the light of his remark that the primary idea of having rules is to save time[4]. There is indeed

[1] Pp. 44–5.
[2] Pp. 43–4.
[3] P. 42.
[4] Or to deal with cases where there is no time: p. 42.

a coherent model of that sort of rule, which I have elsewhere[1] called the 'gas bill' model, which refers to the situation in which the cost to an enterprise of interfering with a fixed process for handling transactions and halting a given item, is greater than a loss which is indeed incurred on that item. That model makes it clear why, for an individual, the value of rules of thumb is costed principally in terms of time. It also illuminates the point that once an agent has perceived the disutility in the particular case, there is no point in his following the rule in that case; for coming to perceive the immediate disutility is the individual analogy to interrupting the commercial process – the reflective intervention which costs the time has already been made.

There are of course cases in which following a 'rule of thumb' will generate more disutility than breaking it. But necessarily, of course, there is no certain way of identifying such cases in advance: for to make sure of each case whether it was or was not of that sort would involve in each case the reflective intervention which it is the point of the rule to avoid. So anyone who adopts a 'rule of thumb' will know in advance that there will be some exceptional cases which will not announce themselves as exceptional cases; that is, he will know that he is licensing some tactical disutility in the pursuit of strategic utility. Now, if the facts are as we have supposed, he will not be able to avoid losing some utility, since the alternative is to consider every case, and considering every case has, in sum, greater disutility. But he will know in advance that some of the actions he will do will not be, by direct utilitarian standards, the right actions, or even, relative to the evidence one could have gathered if one had investigated the particular cases, probably the right actions. Thus there will be a utilitarian type of reason for thinking it better to adopt a course of action which

[1] *Morality*, section on utilitarianism.

involves, one already knows, not always doing the right action.

To accept this last point does not involve abandoning what I earlier called the 'act-adequacy premiss'. One could accept the last point, and still think that all utility-changes in the world were induced via actions; one would merely have to recognize that one's sometimes doing wrong actions was a necessary condition of more optimific actions being done, even by oneself. This is the sort of spirit, perhaps, in which Smart suggests that knocking off good works for a bit might be a means to doing more good works.[1] In fact, I think that that is as far as Smart is prepared to take it, at least when he is thinking strictly in terms of direct utilitarianism as a personal morality: rules of thumb will be acceptable to me in so far as they render it more probable that they will lead to more right actions in the long run being done by me. Moreover, if they are to have that tendency, it is important that I *treat* them as rules of thumb, which means not only that if I do discover that this is an exceptional case, then I treat it as an exception, but also – and importantly – I keep a utilitarian eye open for signs that a case may be exceptional.

But if these precautions are rational, then clearly the utilitarian agent had better not go too far in the direction of cultivating spontaneity or a lack of conscious concern for utilitarian considerations, since every step in that direction must tend to decrease the probability that he will do right actions; unless one believes either that the Invisible Hand of early capitalism will guide the unreflective agent to utilitarianly desirable outcomes, or else that rationally utilitarian deliberation in particular cases is actually harmful to utilitarian outcomes *in those cases* (even apart from loss of time, etc.), which may well be true, but can hardly be believed

[1] P. 55.

by, at least, a direct utilitarian. It is for these reasons, no doubt, that while Smart does make some excursions into licensing non-utilitarian states of mind, he displays some caution in doing so. The relaxing from good works not only will, it is hoped, produce more good works, but is designed to; and if spontaneity has utilitarian value, then doubtless we can organize some spontaneity. That Smart's direct utilitarianism is in fact cautious about commending dispositions which are psychologically removed from the calculation of utilities is suggested also by his saying virtually nothing about excellencies of character which might go into the specification of a good man, or various sorts of good man; and that his account of that notion itself is done entirely in terms of a man's maximizing right actions.[1]

It is consistent of Smart, I believe, to restrict departures from utilitarian calculation, if he is going to be a direct utilitarian; but then it is not consistent of him to present direct utilitarianism as a doctrine merely about justification and not about motivation. There is no distinctive place for *direct* utilitarianism unless it is, within fairly narrow limits, a doctrine about how one should decide what to do. This is because its distinctive doctrine is about what acts are right, and, especially for utilitarians, the only distinctive interest or point of the question what acts are right, relates to the situation of deciding to do them.

In one, and the most obvious, way, direct utilitarianism is the paradigm of utilitarianism – it seems, in its blunt insistence on maximizing utility and its refusal to fall back on rules and so forth, of all utilitarian doctrines the most faithful

---

[1] 'A good agent is one who acts more nearly in a generally optimific way that does the average one' (p. 48). It is not in the least clear what this means, but it does seem to represent a rather relaxed standard: thus the well-known difficulty of finding ten good men in Sodom (Genesis 18–19) should perhaps not have arisen, unless Sodom had an exceedingly small population.

to the spirit of utilitarianism, and to its demand for a rational, decidable, empirically based, and unmysterious set of values. At the same time, however, it contains something which a utilitarian could see as a certain weakness, a traditional idea which it unreflectively harbours. This is, that the best world must be one in which right action is maximized. Under utilitarianism, it is not clear that this claim even has to be true; and when it is true, it turns out more trivial than it looks.

If the act-adequacy premiss is false, the claim need not even be true. Imagine that the greatest utility was in fact produced by people displaying and witnessing spontaneous and zestful activity. Many particular acts would be wrong, in the sense that if these acts were replaced there could be an increase in utility; but there is no way of replacing them without destroying the spontaneity and zest. Here right acts are sacrificed, indeed to greater utility, but not to greater utility which involves any larger number of right *acts* – it lies rather in a certain style and spirit of action. If, on the other hand, the act-adequacy premiss is true, then right action should be maximized, since what will be bought by a system which involves individually wrong acts will be, in this case, a larger number of right acts. But this is a triviality. For even if right acts were being maximized; and even if, further, my act were individually necessary to that being so, so that even this act of mine were, selectively, right: it would not follow that its utilitarian rightness would be evident to me or to anyone else in the situation.

An example, boringly fanciful and schematic in itself, may illustrate the point here. A utilitarian enlightened community might find that there was a tendency among the citizens to slip away from the utilitarian spirit, making reckless decisions themselves, and grumbling about arrangements which scientific enquiry had shown to be for the best. The most painless way of curing this is to find a means to remind them of the disadvantages of not being utilitarian. The government establishes a reservation of profoundly non-utilitarian persons, of Old Testament or other magical persuasion, leaves them to get on with their lives, and by secret means transmits by TV to the rest of the people some of the more richly counter-utilitarian consequences of their way of life. If this worked as planned, the non-utilitarian acts of those in the reservation would in fact be utilitarianly right, or at least some indeterminably large proportion of them would be (the allocation of marginal effects would be impossible); but the way in which they in fact contributed to maximizing utility would be one which required almost everyone outside the reservation to regard them as wrong, and those inside the reservation to regard them as right for reasons which for the utilitarian would make them wrong. Thus even granted the act-adequacy premiss, there is nothing but a triviality in the proposition that right acts should be maximized. It does not follow that one should maximize what seem to utilitarians right acts. It may well be best to secure many of what utilitarians will be bound to regard as wrong acts, and there is no reason why the distribution of these between persons should be equal: as the model illustrates, there might be utilitarian reasons for there being a corner in 'wrong' acts among some particular men. Utilitarianism has no more reason to insist on equity in this respect than in any other.

Once one has moved back in this way to the 'total assessment' position, the utility of anything is open to question, including, of course, that of utilitarian thinking as a personal and social phenomenon. There are some powerful reasons for thinking that its prevalence could be a disaster. Some of these are hinted at occasionally by Smart, at those points at which he wishes (as I have suggested, inconsistently) to keep direct utilitarianism and at the same time spirit away utilitarian calculation. Let me mention two others.

First, many of the qualities that human beings prize in society and in one another are notably non-utilitarian, both in the cast of mind that they involve and in the actions they are disposed to produce. There is every reason to suppose that people's *happiness* is linked in various ways to these qualities. It is no good the utilitarian saying that such happiness does not count. For as we have already seen in this connexion, modern utilitarianism is supposed to be a system neutral between the preferences that people actually have, and here are some preferences which some people actually have. To legislate them out is not to pursue people's happiness, but to remodel the world towards forms of 'happiness' more amenable to utilitarian ways of thought. But if they are not to be legislated out, then utilitarianism has got to co-exist with them, and it is not clear how it does that. As we have already seen with Smart's remarks on spontaneity, you cannot both genuinely possess this kind of quality and also reassure yourself that while it is free and creative and un-calculative, it is also acting for the best. Here we have that same problem of alienation from one's projects which we considered before in relation to integrity.

Second, there is the *Gresham's Law* problem, related to the well-known problem of games theory, the Prisoner's Dilemma.[1] The upshot of the Dilemma (the details of which need not concern us here) is that it can be individually rational for two players in a competitive game to adopt strategies which jointly produce an outcome worse than could have been achieved by their each adopting another strategy; but while they can both see this, neither of them can afford to adopt the different strategy, for fear that he will do so alone, something which would produce a worse outcome for him (though better for his opponent) than any

[1] For a discussion of the Dilemma, see e.g. Luce and Raiffa, *Games and Decisions* (Wiley, London, 1967). The present argument is a slightly expanded version of one in *Morality, loc. cit.*

other. The way out of this is co-operating; one way to that is an 'enforceable agreement', where this can be Hobbesianly interpreted as an agreement with an indefinitely large penalty attached to breaking it. The Dilemma is usually interpreted in terms of self-interested preferences, but a similar structure can arise in a competition between utilitarian agents on one side, and self-interested (or merely opposed) agents on the other. Now society cannot exist without some degree of co-operative and (in Smart's term) benevolent motivation, to some degree internalized, to some degree sustained by sanctions. But the system cannot and does not guarantee peace, both because there are agents who are uncooperative, and also because there are conflicts of view about what may constitute happiness (the utilitarian assumption that it must be possible, by a maximizing function, to combine in some sort of compromise as many people as possible getting as much as possible, just depends on the usual assumptions about the demure and essentially domestic character of what people want).

Once such conflicts cannot be resolved within the usual framework of compromise, utilitarianism has a particular tendency to raise the conflict to new levels. For it must always be the utilitarian's business, thinking as a utilitarian, to take the least bad action necessary and sufficient to prevent the worst outcome: pre-emptive action is of the essence of utilitarian rationality. But since an opponent may know that the utilitarian is a utilitarian and is committed to this, he himself will raise his bid. Both may see, as in the Dilemma, that the joint outcome of these procedures will be very bad, but there is no way in which the utilitarian can cut off the process without taking an unjustified risk with the utilities he is supposed to be maximizing. Thus he is driven on by utilitarian rationality itself to outbid the opponent, and the cumulative process is disastrous, although no particular departure from it can be justified.

Of course the situations in which such conflict can grow are in various ways restricted, in particular within the state, since it is the aim, and if Hobbes is right the function, of state power to contain such conflicts. But there are inter-state conflicts, and conflicts between state power and other forces, and indeed the same structure can apply to conflicts within the state, even if state power suffices to stop the full menu of violent means being explored by the combatants. Moreover, the mere existence of state power is inadequate to contain conflict unless people in the state are to some degree motivated to avoid conflict. Both in the provision of such a motivation, and in the business of limiting potentially limitless conflict, there is reason to think that a distinctively non-utilitarian disposition is needed: a disposition to limit one's reactions, even though in the particular case the cost of so doing may turn out to be high. That is to say, people have to be motivated, and deeply motivated, not to take the means necessary and sufficient to prevent, in the particular case, the worst outcome. A system of dispositions against pre-emptive action – even in the face of strong provocation to utilitarian conduct – has a chance of limiting conflict, and such a system requires people to be brought up and fortified in dispositions not to think of situations in a utilitarian way. This is not to say that they do not think at all in terms of the consequences of their actions – that would be merely insane, if intelligible at all. Nor does it mean they fix one definite limit to their response whatever may threaten, as pacifists do: that would be to suppose that the only alternative to utilitarianism was accepting that there were certain things obligatory whatever the consequences, a position we rejected a long time ago, in section 2. It means rather that the response falls short of what would be utilitarianly required at a given point: and falls firmly and reliably short of it.

Two utilitarian answers can be considered here. The

utilitarian may say, first, that anyone can talk about what would be desirable to limit conflict; no doubt if these dispositions were general, conflict would be contained. But equally, if utilitarianism were general, conflict would be contained. This reply just misses the point of the argument. Let us concede that if utilitarianism were general, conflict would be contained; though in fact, there is some doubt about this, unless one adds that not only do the parties agree on the formalities of utilitarianism, but they share a common, or at least only trivially various, concept of happiness. The point concerns the situation in which not all the parties have co-operative dispositions – that is to say, the actual situation. If one party to a conflict lacks co-operative dispositions, and the other is a strict utilitarian, then the ground is rich for conflict to grow pre-emptively; if the more socialized party has a disposition to resist pre-emption, it may not.

Another utilitarian answer will be that the arguments I have advanced for these dispositions are anyway utilitarian arguments. In a way, that is right, and they are meant to be – they are meant to use utilitarian terms to the maximum degree. But what they show, if correct, is that granted some empirical generalities of a kind which are the background to all problems of morality, utilitarianism's fate is to usher itself from the scene. As we have seen, direct utilitarianism represents certainly a distinctive way of deciding moral questions, a way, however, which there is good reason to think, if generally employed, could lead to disaster; and some qualifications which Smart is disposed to put in seem to signal some recognition of that, and a comprehensible desire to leave the way open for utilitarianism to retire to a more indirect level, towards the dimension of total assessment. But once that has started, there seems nothing to stop, and a lot to encourage, a movement by which it retires to the totally transcendental standpoint from which all it demands is that the world should be ordered for the best, and that those dispositions and habits of thought should exist in the world which are for the best, leaving it entirely open whether those are themselves of a distinctively utilitarian kind or not. If utilitarianism indeed gets to this point, and determines nothing of how thought in the world is conducted, demanding merely that the way in which it is conducted must be for the best, then I hold that utilitarianism has disappeared, and that the residual position is not worth calling utilitarianism.[1]

If utility could be globally put together at all – and that has been an assumption of these arguments, though I shall raise some doubts about it in the next section – then there might be maximal total utility from the transcendental standpoint, even though nobody in the world accepted utilitarianism at all. Moreover, if the previous arguments have been correct, it is reasonable to suppose that maximal total utility actually requires that few, if any, accept utilitarianism. If that is right, and utilitarianism has to vanish from making any distinctive mark in the world, being left only with the total assessment from the transcendental standpoint – then I leave it for discussion whether that shows that utilitarianism is unacceptable, or merely that no one ought to accept it.

7. Social choice

The fathers of utilitarianism thought of it principally as a system of social and political decision, as offering a criterion and basis of judgement for legislators and administrators. This is recognizably a different matter from utilitarianism as a system of personal morality, but it is hard for a number of important reasons to keep the two things ultimately apart, and to stop the spirit of utilitarianism, firmly established in

[1] For a similar view, cf. John Rawls, *A Theory of Justice* (Oxford University Press, London, 1972), pp. 182, 184–5.

one, from moving into the other. If individual decisions on personal matters are made on a utilitarian basis, then those citizens will both direct the same outlook on to their views about what should be done in the public sphere, and also expect the legislature and the executive to make its decisions in that spirit. Indeed, a utilitarian is likely to think that the case for public utilitarianism is even stronger than that for private. For one thing, the decisions of government[1] affect more persons, in the main, than private decisions. But, more than that, he is likely to feel that there is something in the nature of modern government (at least) which requires the utilitarian spirit. Private citizens might legitimately, if regrettably, have religious beliefs or counter-utilitarian ideals, but government in a secular state must be secular, and must use a system of decision which is minimally committed beyond its intrinsic commitment to the welfare of its citizens. Thus utilitarianism can be seen almost as built into a contract of government.

The notion of a *minimum commitment* is an important element in the rationale of utilitarianism, and, if I am right, it particularly applies at the public level. Utilitarianism does in certain respects live up to this promise, in the sense that certainly it rests its judgements on a strictly secular and unmysterious basis, and derives (or at least hopes to derive) its substantial input from what people as a matter of fact want, taking its citizenry as it finds them. But those virtues (to the extent that they are virtues) it in any case shares with certain other systems, as we shall see, which lack some of utilitarianism's characteristic defects. Again, utilitarianism has an appeal because it is, at least in its direct forms, a one-principle system which offers one of the simplest and most

[1] I speak of *government* throughout, as a convenient shorthand for agents or bodies making decisions in the public area. The distinctions between public and private themselves are not meant to be more than extremely rough.

powerful methods possible for eliciting *a* result: its commitment in this regard can also be seen as minimal, in that it makes least demand on ancillary principles. It does, however make enormous demands on supposed empirical information, about peoples' preferences, and that information is not only largely unavailable, but shrouded in conceptual difficulty; but that is seen in the light of a technical or practical difficulty, and utilitarianism appeals to a frame of mind in which technical difficulty, even insuperable technical difficulty, is preferable to moral unclarity, no doubt because it is less alarming. (That frame of mind is in fact deeply foolish; it is even, one might suggest, not very sensible from a utilitarian point of view, but agreement to that may lead once more to the slide in the transcendental direction which we intercepted in the last section.)

The appeal at the social level of utilitarianism's minimal commitments is therefore to some extent not peculiar to it, and to some extent illusory. It is also to some extent real, in the sense that utilitarianism really does make do with fewer ancillary principles and moral notions, but then as critics have repeatedly pointed out, and we shall shortly see, the lightness of its burden in this respect to a great extent merely shows how little of the world's moral luggage it is prepared to pick up. A system of social decision which is indifferent to issues of justice or equity certainly has less to worry about than one that is not indifferent to those considerations. But that type of minimal commitment is not enticing. The desirability of a system of social choice can be considered only relative to what it can reasonably be asked to do, and the simplicity of utilitarianism in this respect is no virtue if it fails to do what can be reasonably required of government, as for instance to consider issues of equity. Certainly the simplicity that utilitarianism can acquire from neglecting these demands is not itself an argument for saying that the demands should not be made.

These are questions that I shall come back to. For the moment, we can note the point that a society disposed to make utilitarian choices in personal morality is very likely to favour utilitarian decision by government, for if they see merit in the first they are likely to see the merit written larger in the second. What about the other way round? The prospect of a society which is utilitarian in government but less so in personal morality is a more recognizable one, and one which lies in a direction favoured by many utilitarian writers. Sometimes it is not easy to tell whether such social arrangements are envisaged by these writers, because a haze hangs over the spot from which the utilitarian assessments are being made, and one cannot see whether the transcendental standpoint has been adopted, and developments in society are being assessed from an imaginary point outside it, or whether, alternatively, a position of utilitarian judgement and decision *within* society is being supposed. Smart's discussion of the utilitarians in a magic society[1] is revealing: they can view society and indeed have an effect on it, but they do not belong to it, and for the best outcome they let the local practices continue. It is not surprising that one should be reminded of colonial administrators, running a system of indirect rule.

If we insist on being told from what actual social spot the utilitarian judgements are being made, and if we form some definite picture of utilitarian decision being located in government, while the populace to a significant extent is non-utilitarian in outlook, then it must surely be that government in that society is very importantly manipulative. For either the government is unresponsive to non-utilitarian demands made on it, and must sustain itself by means other than responsiveness to public demands; or alternatively it has nothing to respond to, because the public's non-utilitarian preferences are directed entirely to private objects. If

[1] Smart, p. 50. Cf. p. 123.

that is conceivable at all, without the public turning out in fact to be utilitarians with non-utilitarian recreations, it will be so only because the government encourages or makes it to be so. In both these cases, the social reality will appear very differently to the utilitarian élite from the way it appears to the ruled. This situation is inherently manipulative, and would very probably demand institutions of coercion or severe political restriction to sustain itself. This is a social and institutional manifestation of that lack of openness which I have already remarked in Smart's proposals.[1] And that is where it has to be written out when utilitarianism returns from the transcendental standpoint to being a political force in society. It is not the ideal observer we have to reckon with, but the unideal agent.

It is worth noticing that the idea of a utilitarian élite involves to a *special* degree the elements of manipulation. It is possible in general for there to be unequal or hierarchical societies which nevertheless allow for respect and decent human relations, so long as people are unconscious that things could be otherwise; but which, once such consciousness has arisen, must inevitably become a different and more oppressive thing.[2] To what extent there are societies genuinely naïve in that sense, is an empirical question, but certainly there could be. But the idea of a society which was ruled by a utilitarian élite and which was naïve in that sense is an absurdity. For utilitarianism is erected on the idea of purposive social action and the alteration of attitudes, by methods and to degrees which only empirical investigation will reveal; and no society whose rulers' outlook was built on that idea could also contain quite innocently the assumption, shared by all, that a division between a utilitarian élite and a non-utilitarian mass was a fact of nature. Individual

---

[1] See section 6, pp. 123–4.
[2] I have said something about this possibility in 'The idea of equality', reprinted in *Problems of the Self*: see p. 238.

utilitarian theorists may manage to be naïve enough innocently to sustain something like that assumption, but no
society could.

I turn now to utilitarian principles of social choice. This is
a very large and technical subject, central questions in which
are at the heart of welfare economics. I shall not try to enter
into these questions.[1] My aim will be merely to produce a
rough map of some of the most important issues, constructed
on the principle of a journey away from utilitarianism.
Starting with the full classical apparatus of utilitarianism, a
range of doubts and criticisms can move one through a
series of stages until one ends with something which is very
little like utilitarianism. An important point about this lies
in the fact that there are several stages. I shall group them,
for the present purpose, very crudely into three steps. The
first is the step from utilitarianism to the recognition that
even using what are, in a very general sense, utilitarian-type
comparisons of utilities, social decision functions which are
not utilitarian are equally possible. This is an important step,
since some of the appeal of utilitarianism to those who want
definite social results rests on the false assumption (not
shared by economists) that utilitarianism is unique in eliciting
a decision from data of this kind. The second step casts doubt
on the adequacy of utilities, perceived satisfactions and
expressed preferences as a total basis for social decision, and
entertains conceptions of welfare or happiness which raise
more pervasive and less definite problems about interpersonal comparison and aggregation. At the third stage,
finally, doubt may break out about the whole enterprise of
having, except for very specific and limited purposes, such
an ambitious and totalistic social decision machinery in any
case; but that is an issue which I shall reach without pursuing.

[1] For a most lucid and helpful account of these matters see Amartya
K. Sen's brilliant book, *Collective Choice and Social Welfare* (Holden-
Day, San Francisco, 1970).

I start with a formulation of Sen's:[1] "In using individual welfare functions for collective choice, there are at least three separate (but interdependent) problems, viz. (a) measurability of individual welfare, (b) interpersonal comparability of individual welfare, and (c) the form of a function which will specify a social preference relation given individual welfare functions and the comparability assumptions." With regard to (a), one issue, which Smart[2] has mentioned, is whether a cardinal or merely an ordinal measure can be imposed; but it is worth noticing that there is no simple relation between the answers to (a) and to (b), since it is not only possible to achieve some forms of interpersonal comparison with purely ordinal preferences,[3] but also it is possible to have cardinal measures of individual preference which do not yield interpersonal comparisons, but which nevertheless admit of solutions to question (c): this is so in Nash's bargaining model.[4]

Classical utilitarianism makes very strong assumptions with regard to (a) and (b), demanding cardinality in reply to (a) and straightforward interpersonal comparisons in reply to (b); it then offers a simple solution to (c), in the form of maximizing either gross aggregate utility, or else average utility, in the simple sense of the aggregate utility divided by the number of individuals.[5] Now it is possible to run versions of utilitarianism on assumptions less strong than these, and though they might lack classical utilitarianism's celebrated ability to yield, in principle, a definite answer for

[1] *Collective Choice and Social Welfare*, p. 118.

[2] Smart, p. 38.

[3] On this, see Sen chs. 7 and 7★, and also Richard C. Jeffrey, 'On interpersonal utility theory', *Journal of Philosophy* 68 (1971) 647–57.

[4] Cf Sen, chs. 8 and 8★.

[5] Smart seems to hesitate between these importantly different alternatives: p. 28. See also Rawls, *A Theory of Justice* (Harvard University Press, Cambridge, Mass., 1972), pp. 162 ff. I pursue one aspect of the 'average' solution below.

all cases, they might win in other respects, as for instance by being rather less unrealistic; while other systems within this general framework, give different answers to (c) which may convey other advantages. As Sen has put it[1] "Such a general framework ... does lack the sure-fire effectiveness of classical utilitarianism, which is one of its very special cases, but it also avoids the cocksure character of utilitarianism, as well as its unrestrained arbitrariness".

I am not concerned here with different bases on which utilitarianism, or some version of it, might be run, nor yet with the details of alternative systems, but merely to draw attention to the existence of alternative systems which, while they themselves pay various prices, can do better than utilitarianism in matters on which it is notoriously weak, above all that of equity. Clearly Rawls's maximin principle – regarded here as a principle for comparing social states, rather than for comparing sets of institutions, which is what he offers it as – satisfies this second condition better than utilitarianism does, though it may give implausible results elsewhere; and more generally, the kind of *lexicographic* ordering which Rawls and others have employed – by which some criteria for preference can be brought into play only after others have been satisfied – is more realistic and sophisticated than utilitarianism's gross insistence on summing everything.

In this light, utilitarianism does emerge as absurdly primitive, and it is much too late in the day to be told that questions of equitable or inequitable distribution do not matter because utilitarianism has no satisfactory way of making them matter. On the criterion of maximizing average utility, there is nothing to choose between any two states of society which involve the same number of people sharing in the same aggregate amount of utility, even if in one of them it is relatively evenly distributed, while in the other a very

[1] *Collective Choice and Social Welfare*, p. 104.

small number have a very great deal of it; and it is just silly to say that in fact there is nothing to choose here. It is not a question, it is perhaps worth insisting, of those who insist on a relevant difference here bringing forward a value, while the utilitarian answer involves no values; utilitarian social decisions involve values as much as any do. Nor can we say that such situations will not arise, because for instance inequity will give rise to discontent, which thus reduces the total and average utility. For the objection to an inequitable state is not contingent on the worse-off persons being discontented; on the contrary, their being worse-off provides a ground for their being discontented, and it is a startlingly complacent and conservative conclusion that it must actually be better if, things being inequitable, people are not discontented.

A moralizing argument in favour of maximizing average utility might be this.[1] The moral point of view is impersonal, and abstracts from one's own personal interests, to look at a situation in a universal spirit. But this comes to the same thing as the requirement that in choosing between social states it makes no difference who in particular one is;[2] and this might be represented as the idea that the social state is best in which a citizen selected at random is best off; and this might be thought equivalent to the requirement that average utility be maximized. It seems in any case extremely doubtful that the consequences of impersonality can be represented just in terms of the utility enjoyed by a randomly selected citizen. But even if it could, the argument is invalid

[1] For considerations in this area, see Rawls, *A Theory of Justice*, pp. 164 ff., though the argument offered here is different from his.

[2] Something of this kind may possibly underlie Smart's flirtation (p. 37) with the idea that under moral impersonality, X's sacrificing X's interests should be seen just as a special case of X's sacrificing Y's interests. Why that result is absurd, and hence why impersonality, if it leads to it, is absurd, are questions closely related to the issues of integrity I have discussed earlier.

as a support to the principle of merely maximizing average utility. For clearly there can be two states of society with population and aggregate utility equal in both, but where the probability of picking at random a citizen whose utility falls below the average is much greater in one than in the other; this will obviously be so for a state in which there is a great segregation of utility to a few persons, since in that case there are many more persons with below average utility than in a state in which distribution is more equitable. The argument gains any plausibility it has from another, and different, application of the principle of insufficient reason: it relies on the fact that out of the indefinitely many social states which display a given average utility, the greater number must be states in which the majority of citizens do not differ from each other in utility by too much. But if that fact supports anything in this area, it can support not the principle of merely maximizing average utility, but that of maximizing it granted that differentials are not too great, i.e. it concedes the case for considering distributive issues.

The next step on the journey away from utilitarianism moves us from issues of how one handles utilities and preference schedules, to the question of whether utilities and preference schedules can possibly be all that we are concerned with, even under the heading of individual welfare. We may pass over, though we should not forget, the gigantic difficulty of discovering even ordinal preferences over even private and homogeneous goods. The present difficulties start from the facts that the goods may not be homogeneous, and they may not be private. The principle of the substitutability of satisfactions is basic to utility calculations; it turns up, for instance, and very evidently, in the Hicks–Kaldor compensation test, to the effect that a change is an unequivocal improvement if its beneficiary is made so much better off by it that he could compensate the loser from it and still have something over. It can hardly be an objection to economics, as economics, that it is about money. But once such principles are seen as *the* principles of social decision, one should face the fact that goods are not necessarily inter-substitutable and consider the case, for instance, of an intransigent landowner who, when his avenue of limes is to be destroyed for the motorway, asks for 1p compensation, since nothing can be compensation. That there must be something which constitutes compensation for a finite loss is just a dogma, one which is more familiar in the traditional version to the effect that every man has his price.

The question arises, again, what objects of preference can be handled by the formulae of social decision. This seems to me a very difficult question, on which not enough is yet known; thus it is far from clear whether games theory can make good its promise to be able to handle any set of preferences, including altruistic ones, without destroying its theoretical basis. We have already met, in section 5, the question of what projects utilitarianism can satisfactorily contain without either collapsing into the evidently restricted and egoistic assumptions of classical Benthamism, or else falling into incoherence about the relations between a man's own projects and the project of utilitarianism itself. In the social field, this same problem emerges once more in the form, particularly, of the question, what degree of social or public content can be allowed to preferences if they are to be straightforwardly part of the input of the social decision function. Groups can hold views about what the state should be like and similar matters of principle or deep concern which they cannot coherently regard as material for a trade-off with other advantages. If they are powerful or determined enough, it is well-known that they can exercise a blocking effect; and structural situations of this kind can lead, for instance, to federal solutions. Now an administrator can view these persons in a utilitarian light, as an obstacle which it costs an indefinitely large amount to remove; but they cannot regard themselves in that light, and certainly one cannot restrict the notion of 'political thought' to the planning which does regard them in that light – their own thought can itself be political thought. So if utilitarianism is to provide the criterion of rational political thought, it follows that no one should, ideally, think as such persons do. That is to say, utilitarianism once more legislates not just to the handling, but to the content and seriousness, of the projects in society.

As we found in the individual case, so in political decision, utilitarianism is forced to regard 'commitments' (as I previously called them) externally, as a fanatical deviation from the kind of preference which can be co-operatively traded off against conflicting preferences. That might seem in any case a gratuitous evaluation, and an impermissible limitation on the supposed topic-neutrality of utilitarianism's view of preferences. But it might be yet worse. For it might turn out, as I have already mentioned, in discussing the individual case, that the happiness of many men – by criteria of happiness which utilitarianism would itself have to recognize – lay in their identification with these commitments, these self-transcending social objectives which do not allow of trade-offs.

Perhaps humanity is not yet domesticated enough to confine itself to preferences which utilitarianism can handle without contradiction. If so, perhaps utilitarianism should lope off from an unprepared mankind to deal with problems it finds more tractable – such as that presented by Smart[1] in a memorably Beckett-like image, of a world which consists only of a solitary deluded sadist.

There is a different radical problem which arises even if we look at preferences of a more immediately domestic character. However elusive the ordinal structure of an individual's preferences is admitted by utilitarians to be, it

[1] Smart, p. 25.

will naturally be taken to refer to what he does now *actually* prefer. Even if this were ascertainable (and ascertainable without interference, which is a further point), it would fall short of an adequate basis for social decision in many cases, because it might not coincide with what the individual would prefer if he were more fully informed, and if he had some more concrete sense of what things would be like if his preference, or various alternatives to it, came off. Considerations of this kind are often rejected as élitist or authoritarian, and the generous employment of notions of a 'real will' by political manipulators certainly provides grounds for a healthy respect for that kind of objection. But nevertheless, and far short of its more contentious deployments, the point has power. For anyone who admits the role of expert consideration in government – and utilitarians are certainly the last to reject it – thereby admits that an uninformed preference may well fail to coincide with what that same individual would prefer if he became informed. Nor can we accept the idea that it is *just* a matter of people's having established desires, and being informed or not about particular outcomes as realizations of those desires. What one wants, or is capable of wanting, is itself a function of numerous social forces, and importantly rests on a sense of what is possible. Many a potential desire fails to become an express preference because the thought is absent that it would ever be possible to achieve it.

None of this provides an alternative formula for arriving at social decisions, nor could it; but it points to a glib illusion which utilitarianism trades on, and which renders utilitarianism irresponsible – the illusion that preferences are already given, that the role of the social decision process is just to *follow* them. There is no such thing as just following. To engage in those processes which utilitarianism regards as just 'following' is – by a style of argument which, ironically, utilitarianism is particularly fond of – itself doing something:

it is choosing to endorse those preferences, or some set of them, which lie on the surface, as determined by such things as what people at a given moment regard as possible – something which in its turn is affected by the activities of government.

In this, we have a special case of something which is very important. A well-known argument of utilitarianism against criticisms of this kind is that we can agree that everything is imperfect – only roughly discovering preferences and aggregating them, supposing that actual and present preferences are the only relevant preferences, giving strongest emphasis to those preferences which we are theoretically in the best position to handle, treating non-substitutable goods as substitutable, and so on: but that, all the same, half a loaf is better than no bread, and it is better to do what we can with what we can, rather than relapse into unquantifiable intuition and unsystematic decision. This argument contains an illusion. For to exercise utilitarian methods on things which at least seem to respond to them is not merely to provide a benefit in some areas which one cannot provide in all. It is, at least very often, to provide those things with prestige, to give them an unjustifiably large role in the decision, and to dismiss to a greater distance those things which do not respond to the same methods. Just as in the natural sciences, scientific questions get asked in those areas where experimental techniques exist for answering them, so in the very different matter of political and social decision weight will be put on those considerations which respected intellectual techniques can seem, or at least promise, to handle. To regard this as a matter of half a loaf, is to presuppose both that the selective application of those techniques to some elements in the situation does not in itself bias the result, and also that to take in a wider set of considerations will necessarily, in the long run, be a matter of more of the same; and often both those presuppositions are false.

At this point we reach the edge of such large questions as: to what extent should political thought be seen as a matter of systematic principles at all? How far can the application of such principles determine more than very abstract models which the urgencies and complexities of actual political life will make irrelevant? What intellectual structures, such as those of lexicographic arrangement, could be applied to such principles? Are important political changes discontinuous in ways which no one authority acting in an administrative spirit could allow for? In what ways can government, and public control over government, responsibly handle the facts that people's preferences are in some part a function of their expectations, and their expectations in some part a function of what government does? These are real questions, not rhetorical ones, and they are some of the more important, though not necessarily the newest, questions of political philosophy. The relevant point here is that on virtually none of them has utilitarianism anything interesting to say at all; they are questions which start after it has run out.

Utilitarianism is in more than one way an important subject; at least I hope it is, or these words, and this book, will have been wasted. One important feature of it, which I have tried to bring out, is the number of dimensions in which it runs against the complexities of moral thought: in some part because of its consequentialism, in some part because of its view of happiness, and so forth. A common element in utilitarianism's showing in all these respects, I think, is its great simple-mindedness. This not at all the same thing as lack of intellectual sophistication: utilitarianism, both in theory and practice, is alarmingly good at combining technical complexity with simple-mindedness. Nor is it the same as simple-heartedness, which it is at least possible (with something of an effort and in private connexions) to regard as a virtue. Simple-mindedness consists in having too few thoughts and feelings to match the world as it really is. In private life and the field of personal morality it is often possible to survive in that state – indeed, the very statement of the problem for that case is over-simple, since the question of what moral demands life makes is not independent of what one's morality demands of it. But the demands of political reality and the complexities of political thought are obstinately what they are, and in face of them the simple-mindedness of utilitarianism disqualifies it totally.

The important issues that utilitarianism raises should be discussed in contexts more rewarding than that of utilitarianism itself. The day cannot be too far off in which we hear no more of it.

Bibliography

The following abbreviations are used:

A, Analysis; AJP, Australasian Journal of Philosophy; APQ, American Philosophical Quarterly; E, Ethics; I, Inquiry; JP, Journal of philosophy; M, Mind; N, Noûs; P, Philosophy; PAS, Proceedings of the Aristotelian Society; PQ, Philosophical Quarterly; PR, Philosophical Review; T, Theoria.

Some editions of important nineteenth-century works on utilitarianism are the following: Jeremy Bentham, *Fragment on Government and Introduction to the Principles of Morals and Legislation*, edited by Wilfrid Harrison (Blackwell, Oxford, 1948), and *Deontology*, edited by John Bowring (Tait, Edinburgh and London, 1843); J. S. Mill, *Utilitarianism, On Liberty, Essay on Bentham, together with Selected Writings of Jeremy Bentham and John Austin*, edited by Mary Warnock (Collins, London, 1962); H. Sidgwick, *Methods of Ethics* (Macmillan, London, 1962); S. Gorovitz has edited Mill's *Utilitarianism* together with many critical essays on utilitarianism in general as well as on Mill in particular (Bobbs-Merrill, Indianapolis, 1971).

An exposition and discussion of Sidgwick may be found in C. D. Broad, *Five Types of Ethical Theory* (Routledge and Kegan Paul, London, 1930). In his *Principia Ethica* (Cambridge University Press, London, 1962) G. E. Moore argued for ideal utilitarianism, as he did in a more popular form in his *Ethics* (Oxford University Press, London, 1965).

Act-utilitarianism and rule-utilitarianism are distinguished from one another and discussed in R. B. Brandt, *Ethical Theory* (Prentice-Hall, Englewood Cliffs, N. J., 1959). For various forms of rule-utilitarianism see: Stephen Toulmin, *An Examination of the Place of Reason in Ethics* (Cambridge University Press, London, 1950); K. E. M. Baier, *The Moral Point of View* (Cornell University Press, Ithaca, N.Y., 1958); M. G. Singer, *Generalization in Ethics* (Knopf, New York, 1961); John Rawls, 'Two concepts of rules', *PR* 64 (1955) 3–32, reprinted in M. D. Bayles (ed.), *Contemporary Utilitarianism* (Doubleday, New York, 1968), in Philippa Foot (ed.), *Theories of Ethics* (Oxford University Press, London, 1967), in S. Gorovitz (*op. cit.*), and in Thomas K. Hearn, Jr. (ed.), *Studies in Utilitarianism* (Appleton-Century-Crofts, New York, 1971); R. B. Brandt, 'Some merits of one form of rule utilitarianism', *University of Colorado Series in Philosophy* 3 (1967) 39–65, and reprinted in Gorovitz (*op. cit.*) and Hearn (*op. cit.*). B. J. Diggs, 'Rules and utilitarianism', *APQ* 1 (1964) 32–44, reprinted in Bayles (*op. cit.*), and Gorovitz (*op. cit.*), is concerned to clarify the notion of a rule which is needed by the rule-utilitarian. Kenneth Pahel and Marvin Schiller (ed.), *Readings in Contemporary Ethical Theory* (Prentice-Hall, Englewood Cliffs, N.J., 1970) includes a not previously published comment by Diggs on Brandt's article (*op. cit.*) as well as the just mentioned articles by Rawls, Brandt and Diggs. Gerald Barnes, 'Utilitarianisms', *E* 82 (1971) 56–64 defends rule-utilitarianism against act-utilitarianism.

On the issue between act-utilitarianism and rule-utilitarianism see also A. C. Ewing, 'Suppose everybody acted like me', *P* 28 (1953) 16–29, A. K. Stout, 'Suppose everybody did the same', *AJP* 32 (1954) 1–29, and D. Braybrooke, 'The choice between utilitarianisms', *APQ* 4 (1967) 28–38. J. J. C. Smart, 'Extreme and restricted utilitarianism', *PQ* 6 (1956) 344–54, contains some serious errors which have been corrected in the revised version which has been reprinted in Bayles (*op. cit.*), in Foot (*op. cit.*), in Gorovitz (*op. cit.*), in Hearn (*op. cit.*) and in Pahel and Schiller (*op. cit.*).

J. O. Urmson has interpreted Mill as being a rule-utilitarian. See his 'The interpretation of the philosophy of J. S. Mill', *PQ* 3 (1953) 33–9, reprinted in Bayles (*op. cit.*), in Foot (*op. cit.*), in Gorovitz (*op. cit.*), and in Hearn (*op. cit.*). Brian Cupples, 'A defence of the received interpretation of J. S. Mill', *AJP* 50 (1972) 131–7, argues against Urmson's interpretation. Also relevant in this connexion is John M. Baker, 'Utilitarianism and "secondary principles"', *PQ* 21 (1971) 69–71. J. D. Mabbott, 'Interpretations of Mill's "utilitarianism"', *PQ* 6 (1956) 115–20, which is reprinted in Foot (*op. cit.*) and Hearn (*op. cit.*).

H. J. McCloskey has been a keen critic of both act-utilitarianism and rule-utilitarianism. See his 'An examination of restricted utilitarianism', *PR* 66 (1957) 466–85, which is reprinted in Bayles (*op. cit.*), in Gorovitz (*op. cit.*) and in Hearn (*op. cit.*). McCloskey's 'A non-utilitarian approach to punishment', *I* 8 (1965) 249–63, evoked a spirited reply by T. L. S. Sprigge, 'A utilitarian reply to McCloskey', *ibid.* 264–91, and both of these articles have been reprinted in Bayles (*op. cit.*). McCloskey replies to Sprigge in his 'Utilitarian and retributive punishment', *JP* 64 (1967) 91–110, and for a more general discussion of utilitarianism, see McCloskey's *Meta-Ethics and Normative Ethics* (Martinus Nijhoff, The Hague, 1969) chapter 7. The same author's '"Two concepts of rules" – a note', *PQ* 22 (1972) 344–8, wittily criticizes the article by Rawls which was mentioned in a previous paragraph of this bibliography, making use of analogies with Australian Rules Football. See also Gertrude Ezorsky, 'Utilitarianism and rules', *AJP* 43 (1965) 225–9. Rawls himself has rejected utilitarianism in his impressive book *A Theory of Justice* (Harvard University Press, Cambridge, Mass., 1972). This book was discussed by

David Lyons, 'Rawls versus utilitarianism', *JP* 69 (1972) 535–45, and by Michael Teitelman, 'The limits of individualism', *ibid.* 545–56, with a reply by Rawls, *ibid.* 556–7.

Utilitarianism of the type which I have called 'Kantianism' is presented by R. F. Harrod, 'Utilitarianism revised', *M* 45 (1936) 137–56, which is reprinted in Gorovitz (*op. cit.*), and by J. C. Harsanyi, 'Ethics in terms of hypothetical imperatives', *M* 67 (1958) 305–16. Some discussion of Harrod's paper is included in Jonathan Harrison, 'Utilitarianism, universalisation, and our duty to be just', *PAS* 53 (1952–3) 105–34, which is reprinted in Bayles (*op. cit.*) and Gorovitz (*op. cit.*).

David Lyons, in his book *The Forms and Limits of Utilitarianism* (Oxford University Press, London, 1965), argues that in its most distinctively utilitarian forms, rule-utilitarianism collapses into act-utilitarianism. This is contested by Gertrude Ezorsky in a review article of Lyons' book *JP* 65 (1968) 533–44. Arguments for the equivalence of act-utilitarianism and rule-utilitarianism (in at least one of its forms) have also been put forward by R. M. Hare in his *Freedom and Reason* (Oxford University Press, London, 1963), pp. 130–6, and by R. B. Brandt, 'Towards a credible form of utilitarianism', in H. N. Castañeda and G. Nakhnikian (eds), *Morality and the Language of Conduct* (Wayne State University Press, Detroit, 1963), which is reprinted in Bayles (*op. cit.*). Brandt's thesis is contested by Allan F. Gibbard, 'Rule utilitarianism: merely an illusory alternative?', *AJP* 43 (1965) 210–20 and by J. H. Sobel, 'Rule utilitarianism', *AJP* 46 (1968) 146–65.

D. H. Hodgson, *Consequences of Utilitarianism* (Oxford University Press, London, 1967), argues that utilitarianism is self-defeating, because in a society entirely made up of utilitarians social conventions like those of truth telling and promise keeping would lose their credibility. (The last three chapters of the book contain applications to the question of the justification of judicial decisions.) Hodgson's critique of utilitarianism is contested by Peter Singer, 'Is act-utilitarianism self-defeating?' *PR* 81 (1972) 94–104, and by David K. Lewis, 'Utilitarianism and truthfulness', *AJP* 50 (1972) 17–19. On the ability of utilitarians to deal with such obligations as to keep promises see Rolf Sartorius, 'Utilitarianism and obligation', *JP* 66 (1969) 67–81, in which Sartorius replies to arguments against act-utilitarianism by distinguishing between obligation and moral obligation. He also replies to one of Brandt's objections to act-utilitarianism. Sartorius argues that moral rules are more than mere rules of thumb in his 'Individual conduct and social norms: a utilitarian account *E* 82 (1971–2) 200–18.

For criticisms of the earlier edition of Smart's monograph, see C. Landesman, 'A note on act utilitarianism', *PR* 73 (1964) 243–7, and S. Gendin,

'Comments on Smart's *An Outline of a System of Utilitarian Ethics*', *AJP* 45 (1967) 207–13. For another criticism of Smart's point of view see M. A. Kaplan, 'Some problems of the extreme utilitarian position', *E* 70 (1959–60) 228–32, with Smart's reply 'Extreme utilitarianism: a reply to M. A. Kaplan', *E* 71 (1960–1) 133–4, and Kaplan's further comments 'Restricted utilitarianism', *ibid.* 301–2.

In Smart's monograph the notion of 'consequence of an action' has been left pretty well unanalysed. This notion is given very careful analysis in Lars Bergström, |*The Alternatives and Consequences of Actions* (Almqvist and Wiksell, Stockholm, 1966), and by Dag Prawitz, 'A discussion note on utilitarianism', *T* 34 (1968) 76–84. There is a reply to Prawitz by Bergström, *T* 34 (1968) 163–70. In his 'The alternatives to an action', *T* 36 (1970) 100–26, Prawitz replies again to Bergström and also discusses the paper by Lennart Åqvist, 'Improved formulations of act-utilitarianism', *N* 3 (1969) 299–323. See also Robert J. Ackermann, 'The consequences' in Richard Rudner and Israel Scheffler (eds.), *Logic and Art: Essays in Honor of Nelson Goodman* (Bobbs-Merrill, Indianapolis, 1972). All these works will be valuable for anyone who wishes to consider how to state utilitarianism in a more precise and rigorous manner.

Anthony Ralls, in his 'Rational morality for empirical man', *P* 44 (1969) 205–16, discusses the problem of whether in a generally non-utilitarian society a utilitarian ought to dissemble about his utilitarianism. He argues for a generally Sidgwickian position on this matter, and contends that this position should not be too upsetting for our feelings about the dignity of men. On negative utilitarianism see R. N. Smart, 'Negative utilitarianism', *M* 67 (1958) 542–3, and the symposium by H. B. Acton and J. W. N. Watkins, 'Negative utilitarianism', *Aristotelian Society Supplementary Volume* 37 (1963) 83–114.

In his 'Utilitarianisms, simple and general', *I* 13 (1970) 394–449, J. H. Sobel discusses from a game theoretic point of view certain practical dilemmas which might arise for a utilitarian. In his 'The need for Coercion', in J. Roland Pennock and John W. Chapman (eds.), *Coercion* (Aldine, Atherton, Inc., Chicago and New York, 1972) pp. 148–77, Sobel argues that coercion is needed in a social system if act-utilitarianism is to produce better results than a system with rules of universal veracity and promise keeping. In *Collective Choice and Social Welfare* (Holden Day, San Francisco, Oliver and Boyd, London, 1970), Amartya K. Sen analyses from the formal point of view utilitarian principles of social decision, and compares them with other candidates.

On the question of assessing utilities see D. Goldstick, 'Assessing utilities', *M* 80 (1971) 531–41, and the papers by Richard C. Jeffrey, 'Interpersonal utility', 68 (1971) 647–56, and by Frederic Schick, 'Beyond utilitarianism', *ibid.* 657–66. R. Eugene Bales, 'Act utilitarianism: an account of right-making characteristics or decision-making procedure?' *APQ* 8 (1971) 257–65, argues that the success or failure of act-utilitarianism as a decision making procedure has nothing to do with act-utilitarianism as an account of what makes right acts right.

Besides the paper by Sprigge already referred to, for useful discussions relevant to the relations between utilitarianism and our ordinary moral intuitions, see R. M. Hare 'Principles', *PAS* 73 (1972–3) 1–18, and 'The argument from received opinion', in R. M. Hare, *Essays in Philosophical Method* (Macmillan, London, 1971), pp. 117–35. Also relevant is Jonathan Bennett, 'Whatever the consequences', *A* 26 (1966) 83–102, which is in part a reply to G. E. M. Anscombe's vigorously written paper 'Modern moral philosophy', *P* 33 (1958) 1–19.

The problem of utilitarianism and unborn generations is discussed by Jan Narveson, 'Utilitarianism and new generations', *M* 76 (1967) 262–72, which is reprinted in Gorovitz (*op. cit.*). Narveson is also the author of a broadly utilitarian work, *Morality and Utility* (Johns Hopkins Press, Baltimore, 1967).

DATE DUE